Yin & Yang

Understanding the Chinese philosophy of opposites and how to apply it to your everyday life

MARTIN PALMER

PIATKUS

This book is dedicated to my dear and much loved colleague, Joanne O'Brien, who contributed Chapter 3 but whose contribution to all that we do is incalculable. She has been yin to my yang and I could never have done what I have over the years without her. Thank you Jo!

© 1997 Martin Palmer

First published in 1997 by
Judy Piaktus (Publishers) Ltd
5 Windmill Street, London W1P 1HF

**The moral right of the author
has been asserted**

*A catalogue record for this book is
available from the British Library*
ISBN 0-7499-1628-1

Edited by Carol Franklin
Designed by Chris Warner
Traditional Chinese illustrations © Circa Photo Library
Feng Shui illustrations by Zena Flax

Set in Sabon by
Action Typesetting Ltd, Gloucester
Printed & bound in Great Britain by
Mackays of Chatham PLC

Contents

Introduction

THE ESSENCE OF YIN AND YANG

THE YIN YANG SYMBOL is one of the best known of all Chinese designs. With its vivid flowing black and white swirls, each with a dot of the other at their centre, it has become one of the most prevalent of Chinese symbols in the West. It captures within it the quintessential essence of balance, harmony and of equality. Each one, yin and yang, gives way to the other in flowing lines and each contains within itself, at its very heart, an element of the other. Here is balance, harmony and equality writ large.

This description is in part true. Ying and yang, female and male, cold and hot, moon and sun, earth and heaven – in other words total opposites – do complement each other. Yet their balance, their equilibrium, is not a passive one. They do not lie side by side in peaceful co-existence. Their balance comes from dynamic tension, from the constant struggle of the one to overcome the other. Their energy, the very life energy of the universe, arises from contest and from combat. They each wish to eradicate the other and be supreme, yet they cannot do this, for the very simple reason that nature, the Tao, has placed a part of the other at the heart of each of them. Thus, as they reach their zenith, they peak and begin to decline, allowing the other to rise. The yang forces of summer heat give way inexorably to the yin of autumn chill. The yin of winter's ice cold must melt in the face of the ascending yang forces of spring's warmth. This is what the symbol of yin and yang is telling us.

It is this tension, this holding together of two opposites, which is so exciting about the Chinese world view – and of such importance today. This view offers, I believe, a way of understanding the world about us and of what is happening to us. It offers a way of understanding the contradictions within ourselves, which can help us to come to terms with and have some degree of control over the forces that ebb and flow around us. For we are all caught in such ebbs and flows, in our relationships at home, at work and with the rest of creation. Yin and yang asks us to look again at how we relate to others, to ourselves and to the environment at a time in history when old ways of thinking are crumbling. Into the vacuum new models are just beginning to emerge – or, in the case of Chinese ideas, re-emerge, not only in their own world but in the wider world as well.

WHERE ARE THE ORIGINS OF YIN AND YANG?

The roots of the yin yang symbol lie far back in the ancient past of China, for in this symbol is captured the essence of Chinese philosophy. As such it has helped define Chinese self-understanding, so to appreciate its significance for us today, we need to understand what it speaks of and what it symbolises.

Yin and Yang are believed to have emerged at the very beginning of time, when the great cosmic darkness and no-thing-ness was split by a flash of lightning. All that was heavy and dark came to be yin. All that the lightning brought vividly to light, was light and weightless and became yang. Since that moment of creation, yin and yang have been the only two cosmic forces in existence. Nothing has life except through them and all that is contains both of them.

Yin and yang are not gods, nor are they good and evil spirits. They simply *are*. And as a result the cosmos *is*.

In the West, we have traditionally seen the world as caught between, even as created by, two forces – good and evil. Thus darkness has been seen as evil because it was the opposite of light which we have culturally decided is good. This dualistic world view has quite literally bedevilled us. It has meant that opposites have traditionally been classified into good and bad – male and female, for example.

In China such thinking has never prevailed. Opposites are morally neutral. They simply exist and reflect the eternal opposites of yin and yang. This is why, in a world which has come to see the dangers and destruction of a world view which sets two forces of good and evil against each other, yin and yang are so important now.

Putting it bluntly, the West needs the model of opposites as equals, without any moral assumptions. We need this to heal the old divisions which created a devil to balance God, white people who had to suppress the dangerous blacks, models of men as good and women as bad. This dualism has scarred each of us reared in the West for too long. Without abandoning our own deepest beliefs, be those Christian, Marxist, Jewish or Humanist or whatever, we can find in the yin yang model a way out of the dualistic world view we have inherited. Yin and yang carry with them no religious implications. They can be used by anyone, regardless of what they do or do not believe. It is perhaps because we in the West have long needed such a symbol, that interest in the yin yang symbol is growing so fast.

LIFE AS A DYNAMIC STRUGGLE

At the heart of yin and yang is a powerful vision of life. For, as we have seen, the balance between yin and yang is not one of mutual friendship. The Chinese understanding of balance is that it arises from handling conflict and tension, difference and diversity, and thereby creating harmony. It is not the absence of such forces. It is not some bland, 'wouldn't it be nice if there was no disagreement, no struggle ...' notion. It is actually about handling conflict and balancing difference.

In our contemporary lives, many of us have had to come

to terms with conflict. Because we have grown up in a dualist world, we have been conditioned to expect that the absence of warfare or violence, anger or aggression is peace. Yet how often have we ever experienced peace as anything more than a fleeting few seconds? The reality is that life is a constant struggle. What we need to learn to handle is the resolving of these conflicts through understanding the intimate nature of our involvement with all around us – even that which we dislike.

If we can come to realise that we ourselves contain within us elements of that which seems most opposed to us, then we might be able to learn to live with ourselves a little better. If we can also see that those most opposed to us contain an element of us within them, then adversaries cease to be so absolute. If we can see problems around us as being capable of changing, as the seasons change, as night changes to day, because this is how life is, then we can live more at ease in a complex world. This is why the yin yang model is of such importance.

Yin and yang open doors to new ways of perceiving and thus of living, for while everything in the universe is made up of both yin and yang – everything being a microcosm of the universe – each living thing has either a yin nature or a yang nature. Thus, while human beings contain within them both yin and yang, men are more yang and women more yin. While the stars and planets are made up of both yin and yang, the sun is yang and the moon is yin. While the landscape is made up of both yin and yang, mountains are yang and rivers are yin.

YIN AND YANG IN YOUR LIFE

Balancing our lives is something we all need to do. This book will offer ideas about how to achieve balance in your relationships and family life; how to look at health issues and understand the power of traditional Chinese medicine and acupuncture. It will help you to appreciate why the yin yang symbol can be found on Chinese food packaging, on the costumes of Kung Fu masters, on Taoist statues and on pillows. Today you can see it on products in supermarkets, in pharmacies, in bookshops, in youth clubs, health clubs and places of meditation and reflection. Now you can find out not just what it means and why it is so ubiquitous, but what it can reveal of you and your world. It opens a door of comprehension leading to greater self-awareness and understanding.

Chapter 1 puts yin and yang into their historic and religious context, arising from the shamanic world view of ancient China. The shamanic wisdom of the past has come to be seen as having much to teach us today. Chapter 2 moves from the cosmic world view of the shamans to this world. A world we have traditionally divided into us and the rest of creation. Yin and yang show a dynamic way to reintegrate ourselves into creation. Chapter 3 continues this theme and shows how the ancient art of feng shui can give you a sense of being part of a wider, greater nature, rather than being apart from nature. You will learn how to direct the flow of ch'i, or life energy, in the most beneficial way.

In Chapter 4 you will see that the understanding of your own body as being composed of yin and yang elements means you can begin to apply simple Chinese remedies. For example, if you are overheated – the yang is too powerful – there are yin foods and drinks which can help you to cool down. By balancing your own innate yin yang mixture through use of yin and yang herbs or medicines, you can seek composure and perhaps regain a sense of ownership over your own body which modern medicine seems so often to destroy or deny.

Chapter 5 draws us into the world of art and explores not just how art is used to depict yin and yang but how yin and yang shape art. In Chapter 6 we look to the future. What difference to our hopes and expectations of the future can the yin yang model make? Could it help us face the uncertainties of the new millennium in a fundamentally different way?

As you come to appreciate this way of looking at the world, a new way of understanding and of relating to it emerges. The world can now be seen to be a fine balance of forces, which you can affect adversely or positively, starting with your own body.

WHAT IS YIN AND WHAT IS YANG?

To help you begin to look at the world this way, here is a simple checklist. Note that traditional thought listed women as 'passive'.

Yin

COLD ice • rain • water • rivers • vegetables (but not all) • scaly animals • animals that crawl such as the tortoise • the moon • autumn • head colds • metal • earth and the earth

PASSIVE women • pools and lakes • floods • trees • sheep • cows • fish • phoenix • snake

DARK night • winter • death • underground • coal • all dark colours • spirits • north

Yang

HOT   steam • sunshine • fire • cooking • the sun •
energy • vibrancy • spiced foods • fevers

ACTIVE   men • engines and machines driven by power
• spring • mountains • earthquakes • fires • dragons
• hairy animals • birds • spices • alcohol

LIGHT   the stars • lightbulbs • heaters • daytime •
summer • the gods • south

1

The Yin of the Rivers, the Yang of the Mountains: the World of the Shamans

SHAMANISM AND THE TWO WORLDS VIEW

THE ROOTS of a world divided between yin and yang, and yet also united through their struggle and comprehended by balance, lie far back in the religious and cultural history of China. They are to be found in the two worlds view of shamanism which underpins the philosophical background of China. Shamanism, arising thousands of years ago in Siberia, spread from there down through China and further south; across Russia to present day Finland; across from Siberia to Alaska; and thus down into North and Central America. We have no idea when it began, but we know that it is at least ten thousand years old because the land bridge between Siberia and Alaska, necessary for the transmission of shamanic ideas to North America, disappeared some ten thousand years ago.

Whatever the case may be, shamanism can lay claim to being the first known world religion, and its impact on China was immense. Indeed, it still is considerable, for shamans are at work in China to this day. In rural areas and on the great sacred mountains, shamans are to be found if you enquire carefully. Today, as for most of the last two thousand years, it is the old, the sick, the infertile and the poor who make their way to the shaman's door. Here they can receive help from beyond in ways that none of the organised religions or states can provide. Three thousand years ago it was rulers, warriors and kings who called upon the services of the shamans. But it is many, many centuries, indeed millenniums, since they were the high priests of the country, and controlled events through their powers and influence.

At the heart of shamanism is a vision of two worlds: the material, physical world which we inhabit, and the spiritual world, far superior to this material one. The gift of the shaman is that he or she can communicate between these two worlds. The shaman can enter a trance through which people can ask questions of the spirit world and the spirit world can talk to or make direct contact with this world. At times maverick, at times benevolent, the spirit world causes much to happen in this world, while this world has virtually no power whatsoever over the spirit world. The shaman thus has to try and negotiate between unequal worlds, seeking a balance between the concerns of the material world and the indifference of the spirit world. The sense of being at the mercy of the spirit world and its capriciousness imbues the shamanic literature of China.

In the famous oracle bones of the Shang and early Chou dynasties (c.1750–900 BC), the questions asked via the shamans to the inhabitants of the spiritual world illustrate only too clearly the dependence of the material world on the goodwill of the spirits. Everything from choosing a new city site to enquiring after health was directed to the spirit world and the answers taken seriously enough to be recorded on the oracle bones. The relative insignificance of humanity is shown by the role the king or later the emperor played in appeasing and thus helping to balance nature (of which more later). It was he and he alone who could do this, for he and he alone could claim to have been appointed to this post by heaven – the divine – itself. Only later, around the 5th to 2nd centuries BC onwards, do ordinary people begin to create rituals and ceremonies of their own, and have the possibility of salvation for themselves. Prior to that there was no role for them for, just as the material world was less important than the spiritual, so their existence was of less significance than that of the king/priest, son of heaven.

REIMAGINING REALITY

Around the 5th century BC there is a massive revolution in religious and philosophical thought. The old unequal relationship between the spirit world and the material world is at first challenged and then overthrown in favour of a new model, which itself is both brought into being by the concept of yin and yang, and does most to further that concept. The revolution is that Chinese belief begins to talk in terms of two equal worlds – the spiritual and the material – and begins to relate to the spirit world on an equal basis. At the same time, Chinese technology is beginning to tame some of the wilder elements of the Chinese countryside and geography, from the great and dangerous yin rivers, such as the Yellow River, to the yang threat of earthquakes and the risk of drought.

One of the challenges to order and balance in ancient China was the consistent invasion by outside tribes into areas which the 'black-headed people', the ethnic Chinese, known as the Han, considered their own. The Great Wall of China was not just a grandiose gesture of a proud people, but an absolutely vital necessity if anything called China could have a chance of surviving.

But if invaders were one threat, the greatest threat was the floods. The early mythology of China is dominated by long-term floods, caused by the Great River, the Yellow River, constantly bursting its banks and inundating the homes and fields of the people. This great curse of China has continued to wreak havoc upon the country to the twentieth century. In the 1930s and 1940s, the Yellow River changed course, and in the process of moving back and forth over an area of some four to five hundred miles, brought floods, death and destruction to millions.

The struggle to control the rivers of China dominates Chinese early myths and legends. The great hero Yu, Controller of the Floods, encapsulates this tradition and provides an interesting link back to the shamans and their world vision.

In the legends of Yu, the last of the major mythic emperors, he is both human and semi-divine, or at least capable of magic and transformative powers. As such he acts as a bridge between the great hero rulers who were often demigods, and the beginnings of human rule.

Yu's father, Kun, is clearly a shamanic figure, for upon his death, hunted down by the gods for failing to stop the floods, he turns into a bear. Yu is then miraculously born and taken into the care of the shamans.

This is of great significance. Shamans usually claim to be able to relate directly to the spirit world through the medium of an animal soul-brother or sister. The shaman is in fact believed to be inhabited by a soul which is part human and part animal. Bears feature throughout shamanic culture as the main means of achieving this twinned soul. Thus for Kun to turn into a bear is a clear sign of a shamanic past to this story. Yu himself also has this ability to turn into a bear.

Yu is thus a figure who brings into his narrative the strand of shamanism. The strand of being to some degree at the mercy of the spirit world as it manifests itself and of linking back to a time when human beings sought to supplicate nature, not control it directly. Yet this is precisely what

Yu then goes on to do. Where everyone else has failed before him, Yu, through a mixture of divine aids and good honest hard work, conquers the floods. He controls nature. Indeed, what the myths and legends most stress is that it is sheer determination which helps him win through in the end.

Here is a figure, capable of turning into a bear, aided by magical beings, who uses sheer will-power and physical strength to defeat the floods. It is a story not just of the defeat of the floods, but of the emergence of a notion that human beings, through their own efforts, rightly applied, could control and affect nature and possibly influence the spirit world as well. This is a long way from the shamanic world view.

The written sources for our stories of Yu start around the 5th century BC. They arise at exactly the time when the old shamanistic world view was beginning to both collapse and to be firmly marginalised. This is a time when Chinese philosophy and belief is beginning to experiment with a vast array of new ideas which put the old shamanistic two worlds model into a new light. Humanity is no longer subject to the whims of the gods or the caprice of the spirit world. Humanity, as exemplified mythically in the stories of Yu, is taking control, in common with the divine.

YIN AND YANG AND HUMANITY

The Confucian Triad

This shift from being at the mercy of nature to attempting some interaction with it is of fundamental importance for an understanding of the Chinese view of how harmony and balance are created. It is the interaction from which yin and yang emerge as a theory. One major strand in such thinking stresses that it is through human action that harmony and balance occur upon earth, and to some degree therefore also in heaven. This strand, which can loosely be called the Confucian strand, emphasises the pivotal role of human beings in the balancing of heaven and earth, of yin and yang, of the very cosmos itself. This leads to the model of the triad of heaven, earth and humanity which is so powerful in Chinese thought and practice. As *The Doctrine of the Mean*, one of the four books of Confucian scholarship, states:

> *Only he who possesses absolute sincerity can give full development to his nature. Able to give full development to his own nature, he can give full development to the nature of other people. Able to give its full development to the nature of people, he can give full development to the nature of all beings; he can assist the transforming and nourishing powers of Heaven and Earth. Able to assist the transforming and nourishing of the powers of Heaven and Earth, he may with Heaven and Earth form a triad.*

We all live in a world where we take control of most aspects of nature, even our own nature, for granted. The shamans lived in a world in which none of this could be taken for granted. Perhaps, in our modern arrogance, we have gone too far in asserting our independence, our control of nature and of ourselves. This is where the middle way of the yin yang model offers us a new way of seeing.

The Taoist Model

There is a second tradition which picks up much of the shamanic world view but gets rid of the 'medium as communicator' role of the shaman. This vision emerged at almost exactly the same time as the Confucian approach. It too ends up with a triad of heaven, earth and humanity but in this model humanity has a very different role to play. This is what might be termed the Taoist model, though those who proposed and developed it would not have known themselves as Taoists.

The Taoist model sees the Confucian triad idea as a disaster. Followers of the Taoist model believe that the role we are called to play is one of inaction and non-interference or, to be more precise, of active inaction – called wu-wei in Chinese. The basic idea behind wu-wei is that if only we would go with the flow, be just a part of the Way of the Tao, we would be fulfilled and content. By struggling against the Tao, against the flow of nature, we create troubles and strife for ourselves.

The teaching of wu-wei is beautifully captured in the two key books of what is sometimes called philosophical Taoism, namely the *Tao Te Ching* and the *Chuang Tzu*.

At the heart of the Taoist vision of being is the teaching of not doing things, but allowing things to follow their own course. Chapter 63 of the *Tao Te Ching* captures this very well:

> *The sage does nothing, and so he never fails –*
> *He holds to nothing, and so never loses …*
> *Whereas the rest of us always seem to mess up our lives*
> *just at the moment when we seem to be succeeding!*
>
> *And so he says: do things wu-wei, by doing nothing*
> *Achieve without trying to achieve anything –*
> *Savour the taste of what you cannot taste.*

Chuang Tzu, writing in the 4th century BC, sees wu-wei as like still water which gives back a perfect reflection, and as emptiness. He sees wu-wei as the essence of yin and yang in that it sees inactive action as a perfect balance of the stillness of yin and energy of yang. Chuang Tzu uses the image of still water as a metaphor for wu-wei. He sees the true sage's heart as stilled. 'Heaven and Earth are reflected in it, the mirror of all life. Empty, still, calm, plain, quiet, silent, non-active, this is the centredness of Heaven and Earth and of the Tao and of Virtue.'

He also uses a wonderful image of active non-action as being like a drunkard falling from a wagon:

> *If a drunk falls out of his carriage, even if the carriage is going very fast, he will not die. He is just the same as others, bone and joints, but he is not injured for his spirit is united. Since he does not realise he was travelling, he has no idea that he has fallen out, so neither life nor death, alarm nor fear can affect him, and he just bumps into things without any anxiety or injury.*
>
> *If it is possible to stay united through being drunk on wine, just imagine how much more together one could be if united with Heaven!*

THE BUREAUCRAT AND THE SAGE: YANG AND YIN IN ACTION

The tension between the interventionist Confucian, official-dom world view and the Taoist, quietist, inactive, meditative world view is well captured in the story of the conversion of Lu Tung Pin from being a bureaucrat to being an immortal.

During the Tang dynasty (618–907 AD), a young and very successful official called Lu Tung Pin was travelling from the capital city of Changan to a new appointment in the provinces. He knew he was destined for high office and revelled in the knowledge of his undoubted rise to fame and fortune. However, as he was still on the lower rungs of the ladder of bureaucracy, he was working very hard indeed, and this left him little time to reflect upon the deeper things in life.

As Lu Tung Pin travelled south from the capital city, he stopped for lunch at a roadside inn. Here he found himself sitting opposite an old and venerable looking man, who was in fact none other than the Immortal Han Chung Li. In

Lu Tung Pin (from an early 19th century woodcut)

discussion, Han Chung Li found that the young man was a deep thinker and one who had about him the marks of a potential Immortal. But Lu Tung Pin had no time for such ideas. He was too busy being successful and being in control of his destiny – or so he thought.

As the two men sat chatting, Han Chung Li allowed the aroma of the warm wine he was drinking to drift in Lu Tung Pin's direction. Gradually the young official found himself falling asleep. As he slept, he had a terrifyingly real dream. He dreamed that he rose swiftly through the ranks of officialdom, becoming more and more powerful until, at a very young age, he became prime minister. For many, many years he and his growing family basked in the glory of his position, and grew wealthy and were content.

Then one day the emperor was turned against Lu Tung

Pin. His fall from grace was dramatic – prime minister one day, an exiled criminal the next. The emperor, having been convinced by Lu Tung Pin's enemies that he was plotting to take over the empire, exiled him to the far north, but not before he had had to witness the execution of his entire family. Alone, cold, terrified, in mourning for his family, Lu Tung Pin's existence could not be more miserable.

Then, to his great relief, he awoke. Yet the impact of the dream remained with him. Realising the folly of the pursuit of power, Lu Tung Pin forsook his beckoning life of power and wealth, and went off into the mountains with Han Chung Li to meditate and to learn the Way of the Tao. Many years later he achieved immortality and became one of the great eight immortals, with his teacher, Han Chung Li.

It is clear from stories like these that the Taoist vision of our place and role in the world, in society and within ourselves is very different indeed from the Confucian model. This contrast, the very yin/yang nature of the two fundamental philosophical standpoints in Chinese thought, is one of the major factors that has helped to create the dynamic harmony which is such a feature of all aspects of Chinese life.

It is perhaps best encapsulated in the traditional actions of the emperor. The emperor made two sets of sacrifices and offerings of prayers asking for forgiveness and help each year. The first set was made at the winter solstice when the yang, fiery, male aspect of life is at its lowest ebb. For these sacrifices the emperor fasted for three days and then processed to the south of his palace – the direction of yang – to the Temple of Heaven – also yang. Here the emperor offered sacrifices and prayers to atone for the actions of humanity which had disturbed the balance; to pray for help in keeping the world in balance, and to assist the yang principle to begin to recover. Thus the emperor was both restoring the order and acting to create the continuity of the order.

At the summer solstice, the emperor went to the north of his city – the direction associated with yin, the female, cool

Emperor
offering
sacrifices

aspect of life – and offered similar sacrifices and prayers to
the earth, at the Temple of the Earth – earth also being yin.
Yet again the emperor's role was to stand before the
universe and to offer sacrifices to atone for the wrongs done
by humanity, to ask for help in the coming year and to assist
the rising again of the yin aspect of life, now at its lowest
ebb. Again, the emperor was supplicant and instrument.

This tension between control and controlled runs as a
fundamental theme throughout Chinese life in its search for
balance and harmony. In effect, the Chinese recognised that
the Confucian approach, without the humility of the Taoist

vision, was too arrogant, while the Taoist approach, without the active aspect of the Confucian vision, was too static. It is the interplay between these which forms the basis for the Chinese world view as lived, breathed and experienced in everything of Chinese life from sex to art, from food to religion. This is the dynamic in human life, of the yin and yang of the universe.

In our own world, the tension lies between those who believe that they can change the world for the better and those who believe attempting this is a waste of time. The insight of many faiths is that what is needed is a dynamic interaction between the two: between humility and pride; between non-action and action; between going with the flow and holding back the tide.

By exploring the many levels and depths of meaning in the yin/yang vision of life throughout the rest of this book, I hope to show you that the Chinese have offered the world probably the best model possible for a dynamic interactive understanding of not just ourselves, but of all that exists.

2

Personal Yin and Yang: Our Harmony with the World

UNLOCKING A DOOR TO YOURSELF

As we have seen, all life, according to Chinese belief, is composed of opposites. Within each of us, as within the cosmos itself, are two forces, yin and yang, constantly seeking to dominate and to control, yet inherently incapable of doing so unless influenced by us. We are a finely balanced and tuned creation which needs to be kept balanced. We are, say the Chinese, the sum total of our combinations of yin and yang. Thus while most men are predominantly yang – male, fiery, active – they also contain a feminine aspect of yin. In some men, this yin aspect may be as much or even greater than the yang. Likewise, while women are predominantly yin, they also contain the masculine yang. Again, this can be as great or greater than their yin. Former British Prime Minister

Margaret Thatcher is in fact worshipped in China today as such a woman of yang.

The balance of yin and yang is something you are born with. But you can then adversely affect this balance. For example men who act too macho risk destroying their yin element. Women who become subservient lose something of their yang. Balance is all.

If you are a woman, you will have more yin than yang. But you need to nourish your yang. Becoming too 'feminine' – for example never arguing or being overly cold or distant are all signs of yin becoming too dominant. Conversely, trying to be and act like men – in terms of aggression or the desire to dominate – can mean an excess of yang. For men the balance appears too often to be lost. Domineering attitudes mean the yin is being crushed or ignored. But a weak will can also be a sign of too much yin.

Yin and yang does assume real differences of temperament and style of working between men and women. It does not mean women can only be carers while men go out to work. That is purely cultural. But it does celebrate very different ways of being which reflect the differences between yin and yang.

Even though, then, we may be predominantly yin or predominantly yang, we are also a mixture of both yin and yang, constantly changing and struggling within us. Ill health, colds or fevers, are signs of this struggle having got out of hand within us. If we allow either the yin or yang to overstep a certain point within us, we are subject to forces which unbalance us. This is why Chinese medicine has always placed such a stress on whether you are innately a yin, cool person, or a yang, hot person.

All life is involved in this finely-tuned balance between yin and yang. One of the most famous descriptions of this is contained in *The Yellow Emperor's Classic of Internal Medicine*, which dates from around the 3rd century BC:

> *The Yellow Emperor said: 'The principle of yin and yang is the basic principle of the entire universe. It is*

*the principle of everything in creation. It brings about
the transformation to parenthood; it is the root and
source of life and death; and it is also found within the
temples of the gods ...'*

All life is pervaded with, indeed, made capable of life
through the powers of yin and yang, from the cosmos itself
down to the tiniest speck of dust. In the eyes of the Tao, the
tallest mountain is the same in nature as the lightest feather,
for all are simply the interaction of yin and yang. This is
why, in Chinese belief, the entire universe is found
contained in miniature within your own body and self. Not
just the physical universe either, for all the gods and
goddesses are also present within you. 'You are the universe
and the universe is you,' is the claim made by Chinese, in
particular Taoist, thought.

To understand this is to unlock a door to yourself. In
Chinese belief, your body is a map of the basic elements of
the universe; of the sacred mountains of China, of the interaction between heaven and earth, and as a residence for the
gods and goddesses of the universe! This is hard to comprehend, but hanging opposite me as I write is a diagram of the
human body from the Taoist temple of the White Cloud in
Beijing. The head, spine, heart, bowels and lungs are clearly
visible. Yet they look more like an ancient pathway through
vast mountains, ascending to a great summit – the head.
Seated, standing, running, travelling up and down this
pathway are gods and goddesses. Each is concerned with a
particular part of your body.

So we have a world within. We are a template of the
universe. To understand ourselves we need to know how the
universe of yin and yang, of heaven and earth, of gods and
goddesses works. But, conversely, you can also argue that as
you come to understand the ups and downs, hopes and
fears of your self, of your own body and being, you come to
understand the universe. The two are so interwoven as to be
indistinguishable.

So what is the universe – and therefore you – made of?

THE FIVE ELEMENTS

The Chinese model of existence is based upon the five elements, of wood, fire, earth, metal and water, which are believed to form all material life. The relationship between these five is yet again one of competition and conflict from which emerges the energy of existence. This is well expressed in the following quote from the Confucian scholar Tung Chung Shu of the 2nd century BC:

The vital forces of Heaven and Earth join to form a unity, divide to become the yin and yang, separate into the four seasons, and range themselves into the five elements. 'Elements' in this case means activity. Each of the activities is different, therefore we speak of them as the five activities. The five activities are the five elements. In the order of succession they give birth to one another, while in a different order they overcome each other. Therefore in ruling, if one violates this order, there will be chaos, but if one follows it, all will be well governed.

The inter-relationship of creating the other and of being overcome by the other is a good example of the struggle/harmony model in Chinese thought. The five elements begin in spring with wood and flow through the year, culminating in the winter with water. Each one gives rise to the next, thus:

from wood comes fire,
from fire comes ashes for the earth,
from the earth come the ores containing metal,
from the forging of metal comes condensation and
    water.

But they also oppose each other and can destroy another element. So:

fire is overcome by water,
water by earth,
earth by wood,
wood by metal,
metal by fire.

It is the dynamic of their potential creativeness and their potential destructiveness which gives the five elements their place in the struggle for existence from which existence itself emerges.

As with yin and yang, all life contains all five elements. In some forms of life, one or other of the elements is foremost, but none is in total control. They need each other. Just as they are present in the whole universe, they are also present in us. Again, we contain within us, in miniature, the very essence of the nature of the universe. And again, while we contain all, we are also predominantly of one element or another.

What Element Are You?

- If you are predominantly a water type person, you have a rounded body, smoothly shaped and well padded – but not necessarily fat! Your skin will be soft, full of colour and slightly oily.

- A fire person has a long head and wide chin. Your skin is red and shiny and your hair brown or red. Your bones and sinews stand out clearly.

- A wood shaped person is thin, tall and straight, with strong joints. Sometimes your skin has a greenish tinge. Your fingers are long and knotted in appearance.

- A gold or metal shaped person has a square build and a bright complexion. The bones and muscles are well developed.

- An earth shaped person has thick and heavy features. Your skin has a golden yellow tinge, and overall you are thickset and muscular.

Having said all this, when combined with other elements, these basic types can take on different meanings. A good explanation of this is to be found in *Chinese Face and Hand Reading* by Man-Ho Kwok and Joanne O'Brien (see Bibliography).

WE ARE THE UNIVERSE AND THE UNIVERSE IS US

Because we contain the universe and the universe contains us, Chinese belief stresses that for us to be in harmony and balanced, we need to have the whole world around us in harmony and balance. Likewise, if we are not in harmony and balanced within ourselves, the whole universe is put out of order. We are one and the same thing in our very differences. The well-being of one is inherently caught up in the well-being of the other.

So, if we are becoming too yin, we will increase the yin factor in our own environment and this in turn changes the balance on earth, which affects the universe. Conversely, if the universal balance between yin and yang is upset, then the earth is affected and floods or fires break out and we are then adversely affected. Hence the ritual role of the emperor which we saw at the end of chapter 1, of maintaining a careful balance personally and cosmically. The emperor has gone now, so it is up to each of us.

In certain ways, aspects of the chaos theory, whereby the tiniest change in one part of the world can trigger massive changes in other parts of the world, makes perfect sense to the traditional Chinese world view. The idea that one seemingly insignificant action, such as the flapping of the wings of a butterfly in the Amazon, can set in motion a chain of consequential events, which ends up with a hurricane in Europe, fits well with the principle that the actions of any one of us could upset the delicate balance of life.

This perspective – that we are the universe and the

universe is us – has led to the development of the distinctive Chinese arts of landscaping, building, indeed its whole interaction with nature, with human society, and through ritual with the gods, goddesses and the divine order. Nothing is separate. To make a separation is to introduce a false vision and to begin the process of deception which itself leads to a distorting of the universe.

We are, at one and the same time, one leg of the triad of heaven, earth and humanity, central to the stability of change in the entire universe, and we are also just one aspect of the Tao manifest in this physical world – on a par with mountains and insects, for we are all the same.

It is an awe-inspiring vision, for it both humbles and elevates us at the same time. It shows us how central we are to the whole of existence and yet how little we are. Again, it is a dynamic relationship, and one that offers no simple one way forward.

So, the question to ask yourself is, 'Who am "I" in the Chinese vision of harmony and balance?'

WHO AM 'I'?

'I' am yin and yang in conflict and in unity that is fought over. 'I' am the five elements, generating each other, yet bordering on destruction. 'I' am the original breath which brings the elements and the forces of yin and yang to be – the ch'i or energy which starts off the process. 'I' am a tiny part of the universe; 'I' am the universe. 'I' am the result of what has gone before; 'I' am the cause of all that will come after. Through 'me', all life is sustained, or through 'me' all life is threatened.

In other words, the role of 'I', of 'me', is both individual and cosmic. This is what lies at the very centre of the Chinese perception of 'me'. Think again about the emperor and his role in the cosmos described in chapter 1. Like him, 'I' am both supplicant and controller; both penitent and creator.

Who 'I' am is a fusion between that which is and that which 'I' do. This is clearly brought out in Chinese concepts of fate. In Chinese belief, there are certain things which are given at your birth. These cannot be changed with the exception of your sex – a clear case of adding more yin or yang. They are:

> *when you are born,*
> *whether you are male or female,*
> *whether your family is wealthy or not,*
> *the general state of your health.*

Beyond these factors, nothing else is fixed. It is true that given certain ways of behaving and certain personality traits, fortune-tellers can often predict other aspects of your life, but you are always at liberty to change the way you behave and indeed even to play down or build up certain traits. In other words, your fate is essentially in your hands, though you have been given a certain deck of cards to begin with. If you decide not to try and change, then you will follow a certain course which any perceptive fortune-teller could foresee. But if you take control of your life, if you improve your personality and change the way you behave, you can change who and what you are. This reflects the same model of tension between one way and another. This is the potential for both good and for evil, or the potential for action or inactivity, which runs throughout Chinese thought.

So, who 'I' am is in part up to me. If I decide to continue to be cold and arrogant, hard and brutal, I shall be exploiting the yin aspects of myself. This will be likely to lead to loneliness and to bitterness, which will probably shorten my life but leave me feeling I owe no one anything. If I develop the warm-hearted, open-handed, 'easy come, easy go' aspect of my personality, then the yang aspect of who I am will come to the fore and I shall perhaps live longer, be content with the warmth of friendships and never particularly stand out from the crowd, but nevertheless get most of what I want.

LIFE AFTER DEATH

This interaction between fate and fortune is exemplified also in the various beliefs in life after death. At one level, Chinese belief teaches that you become an ancestor and are worshipped, revered and have influence over your family on earth. You join the greater family of which the family on the physical plane is but one small element. So, you become part of something much greater and, much more important than who you are, is who you are part of.

But another set of beliefs says that you are the sum total of what you have done and that, at death, you will be judged and will have to pay for the crimes you have committed

The fate of souls being recorded in the *Register of Life and Death* in the First Court of Hell

before you can be reborn. Your very rebirth is itself a reflection of what you have made of yourself, for if you have lived a corrupt and degenerate life, you will be demoted in your next rebirth – possibly into an animal form. In this system, you are you and there is nothing else that affects you but you.

So you are part of the flow and thus relatively insignificant, *and* a lone individual creating your own karma and destiny. How can it be that you hold both together? By the simple device of having two souls – the hun and po – the hun soul being yang and ascending to heaven, while the po is yin and remains earthbound. Even at death the tension between the two worlds continues, and throughout it all flows the Chinese notion that this diversity and difference is in fact normal.

That difference and diversity are inherent, and that even 'I' am diverse and made up of conflicting elements, is fundamentally important in Chinese thought.

UNITY OR DIVERSITY: WEST AND EAST

Contrast this belief in inherent diversity with the classic Western position. In the West we have been obsessed for centuries, indeed for millennia, with the desperate desire to make everything one and united. Whether through religion in the form of much of historic Christianity, or political ideologies such as Marxism or capitalism, or humanitarian movements such as the environmental movement, or intellectual systems such as psychology, the West has tried to find one model which explained, held and handled all things. Where these systems have encountered different or diverse models they have tried to ignore, suppress, ridicule or eradicate them.

The Example of Christianity

Let's look at Christianity as just one example, though what can be said here applies to all the other systems listed above.

Christianity, particularly in its Western, that is to say non-Orthodox forms, has attempted for much of its history to get rid of religious and conceptual difference. Only in recent years has this form of Christianity begun to explore the possibility that diversity, far from being a mistake, might actually be how God works, not just in creation, but in the human mind as well. This possibility has been forced upon Christianity by the failure of its attempt to clear up and end all other religions. At the start of the twentieth century, even quite wise Christian leaders were forecasting that the whole world would be Christian by the end of the century. What has actually happened is a vast renewal of many of the other religions, reacting to the imperialism of Christianity; a reforming of Christianity away from the old imperial model and the rise of many new religious movements incorporating elements of Christianity with elements of other traditions, such as indigenous African beliefs. In other words the push for unity, for Oneness, has led to even greater diversity.

The Example of Communism

A similar picture emerges when looking at Communism. In the 1920s and again in the late 1940s it looked as if Communism might sweep across the world, thus eradicating all other political systems and ideological beliefs. This was certainly what many Marxists and Communists inside and outside the Communist countries thought and worked for. What has actually happened has been the total collapse of much of world Communism and much of the political credibility of Marxism as a system, and the emergence of a vast array of new countries, political parties and beliefs in the wake of its collapse.

Recognising the Truth

The truth is that diversity is a natural part of life. This is what some Christians are recognising. If God works through evolution to create, and if evolution can only take place successfully if there is a vast variety of species, then perhaps God also works through the diversity of concepts, beliefs and cultures.

This is not news to the Chinese. They have known that diversity is the essence of the world for many, many centuries. They have managed to live with at least three distinct belief systems – Confucianism, Taoism and Buddhism – using that which is helpful from each whenever necessary and often combining all three. They have existed in a world of two opposing yet intimately interconnected opposites – yin and yang. They have come to terms with an existence both cosmic and individual which contains elements which both create together, and destroy each other.

The role of the individual in this diverse world of difference is both central and peripheral. Let us start with the central aspect.

You as the Centre of the Universe

By what you do and what you do not do, the world is. That is to say, if you act in ways which disturb the balance of yin and yang; if you set one of the five elements at odds with another, then you alter the very nature of the balance of nature. As we have seen, it is like an old, old version of the chaos theory.

At the most local level, the balancing was, and still is, done through the liturgies and actions of Taoist believers and priests. Through cosmic liturgies, Taoism continually repairs the relationship between heaven, earth and humanity. These liturgies are complex rituals of apology and balancing. They are done to control the excesses of human behaviour, as well as the excesses of yin and yang, of heaven and earth, which after all are each out to overthrow the other.

Through fascinating and elaborate rituals, the powers of yin and yang are returned or restored to their rightful places, and to their rightful areas of responsibility or control. Through the actions of the faithful, by offering of incense, by performing of rites, the forces inherent within the world are worshipped and placated, given their rightful place in the order of things. And all this can only be done by humanity. No other force can sustain and repair the balance. This is humanity's unique role in the cosmos – hence our position as one of the three legs of the triad of heaven, earth and humanity.

A Balancing Experiment

For a practical illustration of these ideas try a small experiment. Think of some aspect of your own life which seems out of balance. For example, it might be your health – you are tired and lacking yang energy. Or you might be involved with a bad relationship, which is frustrating your yin, calm aspect. Try meditating on this. Start by washing – not because it has any mystical purpose but just because it will help you to feel relaxed and refreshed. Then dress in something loose, leaving off your shoes. Find a comfortable chair or cushion and sit so you can be at ease. Sitting crosslegged has no spiritual significance so only adopt this position if it is the most comfortable position for you. Focus on your breathing in and out and try to forget everything else. Then slowly introduce to your mind the problem to be confronted. Focus upon this now and call into your life the correcting influence of some aspect of nature which is the yin or yang influence you need, for example the cool calmness of the yin moon or the energy of a yang fire. Try and feel at one with this as you sit and contemplate.

Now turn outwards. Think of a problem in the world – for example, warfare as an excess of yang, or starvation as an excess of yin. Take the influence you have used to help balance yourself to this crisis or disaster. Try and think what you could do to change this destructive imbalance. Finally, return to the influence you have chosen and see what you can give to it.

For instance, imagine you are involved in a destructive relationship – too much yang and not enough calm, cool yin. Draw down the yin power of the moon or draw upon the yin energy of the earth. Focus upon this, and seek insight and calmness from either of these vast yin forces. Once you can feel a sense of the yin rising within you, use it to examine the yang nature of your personal crisis or difficulty.

When you feel you have gained a sense of rebalance there, consider a world crisis. For example, think of a place where warfare rages and bring the influence of the yin of the moon or the yin of the earth to bear upon this crisis. Think of how a cooling of tempers and the ending of revenge could make a difference. Hold the lives of those affected by this war in your mind and in your heart and, depending upon your own religious tradition, pray for them. Then stand back. What can you do to bring a yin influence to bear? You can write letters, send aid, work with groups seeking conflict resolution or defending human rights, pray, get others to pray with you. Perhaps you can exert a yin influence by being still, by not buying things, by not investing in certain companies. By wu-wei (actionless action) as much as by action, there are many ways you can bring your yin influence to bear.

Finally, turn all this back to the yin influence you chose – the moon or the earth. What is your relationship to either of these? With the earth, what do you do that could damage the yin power of the earth? With the moon, your personal involvement will be slight – unless you are a space explorer! So use the moon as a metaphor for otherness, for that beyond what you know.

This is how, in today's world, these ancient liturgies can offer a way of seeing, living and praying, which takes us into ourselves and out of ourselves in a search for the balancing of all life.

This is powerful stuff, so give the exercise time and don't expect to master it quickly.

RIGHT THOUGHT, RIGHT ACTION: BALANCE IN OUR LIVES

Another dimension of the role of humanity in the triad is for each of us to have a correct balance between the forces within ourselves. If one aspect of our being gets out of control or becomes more powerful than it should, our whole being falls apart or is distorted. If we indulge too much in drink, thus increasing the yin within us, we become unbalanced; or if we gorge ourselves on food, thus stoking the yang within us, we likewise become unbalanced. Upon this hangs all the Chinese theories of health, well-being and personality.

Further, if we are out of balance, then, as the whole universe is found within us, the universe is also out of balance. So humanity has to be balanced in order to balance the cosmos.

This theory of the universe being within us and we within the universe is well put in the following quote from the 2nd century BC text, the *Book of Master Huai Nan*:

The heavens have four seasons, five elements and nine divisions with 366 days. Man also has four limbs, five viscera, nine orifices and 366 sections.
Heaven has wind, rain, cold and heat;
Man too has a 'taking in' and a 'giving out'; joy and anger.
Thus the gall corresponds to the clouds; the lungs are vapour breath; the liver is wind; the kidneys are rain and the spleen is thunder.

The Arts of Leadership: the Yin and Yang of Power

In Taoism, the shamanic notion of control and of integration into the spirit world or the superior world dominates. In Confucian thought, the need to be in balance with and to work with the flow of nature, the Tao is foremost. The whole art of Chinese leadership and rule was to be in harmony with and thus able to utilise the flow of time and the course of nature. This is expressed in the following quote from the 4th century BC text, the *Chi Ni Tzu*, where the King of Yueh asks the sage Chi Ni whether natural phenomena have diabolical or auspicious meanings for humanity:

> Chi Ni answered, 'There are the Yin and the Yang. All things have their chi-kang. [i.e their fixed positions and motions with regard to other things in the web of nature's relationships]. The sun, moon and stars signify punishment or virtue, and their changes indicate fortune and misfortune. Metal, wood, water, fire and earth conquer each other successively; the moon waxes and wanes alternately. Yet these normal [changes] have no ruler or governor. If you follow it [Heaven's Way] virtue will be attained; if you violate it there will be misfortune ... All affairs must be managed following the course of Heaven and Earth and the Four Seasons with reference to the Yin and Yang. If these principles are not carefully used, State affairs will get into trouble.

This is echoed in the *Tao Te Ching*. This central text of Taoism differs from many later Taoist texts in being a guide for action, albeit action which is often wu-wei – actionless action. It embodies the idea that the best ruler is one who rules effortlessly by being in harmony with the rule of nature. This is well expressed in chapter 3:

If the sage refuses to be proud,
Then people won't compete for his attention:

If the sage does not buy treasures
Then the people won't want to steal them:

If the sage governs with vision
Then his people will not go wrong.

The sage always makes sure
that the people don't know what he's done,
so they never want to be in control –
and are never driven by ambition.

He keeps them in truth like this
                    acting invisibly.

You see, if there is nothing to fight for
then there is nothing that can break the flow.

A PERSONAL WAY

Now that the emperor has gone, we have to fulfil his former role of balance. Quite simply the above quotes set out a personal way of integrity and of going with the flow. They contain a model of how to live. I have tried to summarise this in the following poem:

You are part of nature and nature is part of you.
Do not try to live as if you are separate.
You are not.
You are part of your family.
You are part of your landscape.
You are part of the seasons.
You are of both heaven and earth.

In their turning,
in their sequence,
is your pattern.

Do not go against the flow of life.
The joys of summer give way to the chill of winter.
But both are necessary.
The solidity of earth enables you to reach up to heaven.
One without the other makes no sense.

If you are hard, hard things will befall you.
If you are soft, you can bend and survive.
If you compete, the world will take you on.
If you are able to be content,
the world will roll on with you.

Be known for what you are,
and make your actions signposts that reveal this.
Flow like water round obstacles.
Do not batter your head against a brick wall.
Flow under it and when it collapses, you will be long
gone.
Act as if you were part of the pattern of the seasons,
of the pattern of day and night.
Be natural, be in nature and allow nature to be in you.

If you keep these ideas before you, you may find that you
can better handle the yin and yang tussle of your own life,
and of life around you. It is a wisdom distilled from millennia of Chinese life, thought, action and wu-wei.

CHANGE AS THE ONLY CONSTANT

One last aspect of Chinese wisdom needs to be mentioned
here and that is the understanding that change is what life
is about. Change is the only constant feature of existence.
So much unhappiness and frustration comes from those
who try to hold on to that which is passing, dying or gone.
Learn to let go.

The *I Ching*, one of the most influential books of Chinese practice in fields as diverse as statecraft to painting (for more, see chapters 4 and 5 of this book), is itself an interesting example of this shamanic, cosmic world view of change. The whole origin of the *I Ching* – the name means the *Book of Changes* – is in the desire to act in accordance with the way or flow of nature, and thus to ensure success and change, but change within the framework of the never-ending change which is life.

Long before either Confucius, Lao Tzu or the Buddha had any impact upon the Chinese, the *I Ching* was shaping awareness and understanding of the world. The *I Ching* is probably the oldest fully extant Chinese divination text. Much of it was created in the 11th century BC and it was probably in its current form by the 9th century BC at the latest. Its origins lie in the history of the rebellion of the Chou tribes against the Shang dynasty in the 11th century BC. Guided by oracle readings given by shamans upon the sacred Chou mountain of Chi Shan, the *I Ching* was originally called the *Chou I – The Changes of Chou*. This marks its historical origin. It was almost certainly used as a key liturgical and dramatic text at the annual re-enactments of the successful conquest, held each year at the Chou ancestral temple. As such it formed the sort of epic, historical, mythological narrative by which the Chou defined themselves – in much the same way as the Exodus story in the Bible shaped and defined Jewish identity (see Joshua, chapter 24) or the Trojan Wars defined Greek identity (see Homer).

However, over the centuries, the *I Ching* with its strange, cryptic oracle pronouncements came to be seen as symbolising and speaking for not just the Chou and their conquest, but also for the struggle to be human. It was seen to refer to the search for balance and order in a world of disorder. It was this aspect which, with the collapse of the Chou dynasty in the 8th century BC, survived the particular identification of the text with historical events. By the time we reach the Han dynasty (starting in 206 BC), the book is no longer known by its historical title as the *Chou I*. It is now called simply, yet powerfully, the *I Ching*, the *Classic of Changes*.

By the time of the Han dynasty, the *I Ching* has become a handbook to everything from art to military manoeuvres. Its role as a key determinant of values and its provision of symbolism to the Chinese world is without parallel. And all of this has occurred without any overt religious dimension, for the *I Ching* is devoid of almost all religious imagery. It is primarily concerned with relationships, and with the yin yang aspect of the polarity between the yin lines and the yang lines.

The core of the *I Ching* is its use of eight trigrams – sets of three lines (trigrams) combining yin broken lines – – with yang unbroken lines —. By adding yin and yang lines together in every conceivable combination of three, you arrive at eight trigrams. The hexagrams come from adding together two trigrams. The maximum number you thus arrive at is sixty-four hexagrams (see pp. 96–101).

The trigrams are supposed to have been revealed to an ancient semi-human, semi-divine being known as Fu Hsi. He was probably a great shaman ruler in the earliest history of China. The trigrams – each of which is rich in associations with directions, elements, stars, colours and yin and yang (the straight line is yang, the broken yin) – were revealed, according to legend, on the shell of a turtle which crawled from the Yellow River to the feet of Fu Hsi. In fact, the lines probably originate with the classic method of fortune telling and oracle divining – heating turtle shells and then 'reading' the cracks that appear. See chapter 5 for how to take a reading from the *I Ching*.

It is perhaps the issue of change that most captures the dilemma of life which the yin/yang polarity of Chinese thought emphasises. Because the Chinese model of reality is one of conflict, struggle, opposition, diversity and difference, it is not a static one. Many cultures seek to return to or create a static world – one in which there is no violence and no struggle. Yet this is doomed to failure because life just isn't like that. The Chinese know better. They know that change is the very essence of existence. What was sure yesterday is gone today. What you plan today will be meaningless tomorrow. With a dynamic model of struggle and conflict, but with an inner assurance that out of this forceful co-existence comes a dynamic harmony and a tense balance, Chinese social, political, religious and even psychological thought has been able to handle and understand change better than most cultures.

The illusion of permanence is something that China has rarely suffered from. The cycle of change exemplified in the *I Ching* is fundamental to Chinese thought, and to Chinese understanding of what harmony and balance mean. To strive for harmony and balance is not to arrive eventually at a place and time when all struggle ceases. It is to be constantly seeking to sustain the drive and drama of life in such a way that, far from standing still, or ending up in a place of absolute certainty, you can actually become part of the ever onward rushing flow of the Tao. The very image of Tao illustrates this, for it is nothing more nor less than the Chinese word for path or road. And roads have a habit of going on and on, into the horizon, ceaselessly changing as they go.

So take this principle of change to heart. Look at your own life. What are you clinging on to? What upsurge of yin or yang have you tried to hold fast to as an expression of normality, when in fact it is an aberration? Can you learn to let go and to flow with the stream of change which washes all away? If you can begin to follow this way, then you are coming close to understanding the true depth of the world as seen through the eyes of yin and yang.

3

Understanding Feng Shui: Harnessing your Health, Wealth and Prosperity

ONE OF THE MOST well-known applications of yin and yang and the search for harmony is the art of feng shui. In this ancient art, the Chinese have sought to bring together the yin and yang of the landscape – the yin of rivers and streams, pools and lakes, with the yang of the mountains, forests and hills. From the vastness of cities to the minutiae of your own living room, feng shui is the practical art of living and developing in relationship with the yin and yang of your surroundings.

Feng shui literally means 'wind and water', and refers to the powerful shaping effects of these elements upon the landscape. Feng shui is based on the principle that we are surrounded by hidden and visible forces that shape and control our lives. The skill of the feng shui experts lies in their ability to sense the balance of yin and yang, and the flow of ch'i in relation to a building and its surroundings.

Ch'i is the life breath or energy which is in all things and it is continually on the move, being channelled swiftly or slowly, gathering or dispersing, flowing through people and the landscape.

FENG SHUI IN THE LANDSCAPE

The Chinese landscape is a reflection of the Tao, where everything flows according to a natural order and has an innate harmony. Deep yin valleys are counteracted by towering yang mountain peaks, arid yang planes are balanced against low-lying yin marshland, and windswept hills against verdant forests. Because of its diversity and grandeur the Chinese landscape has always been a favourite subject of Chinese artists, and among all the natural elements water and mountains have most captured the artistic imagination.

As well as depicting their own inherent natural harmony, the mountain/water landscape in Chinese art also represents the relationship between heaven, earth and humanity. The mist-shrouded pinnacles and peaks reach towards heaven, the ultimate force in the universe. Mountains are often rocky and exposed to the elements and, as such, are a strong source of yang. Here lies the energetic source of the streams and waterfalls that flow down their slopes. Coming down the mountain the slopes are less steep, trees and shrubs appear, and temples or feng shui towers (small pagoda-like towers which either concentrate or discharge power in the landscape) may be dotted about. In some places the flow of the water may be gaining strength, while in others its flow is calmed by pools or hollows. The harsh yang of the windswept peaks is tempered by the yin of calmer waters, secluded hollows and shady groves. Further down the mountain the slopes begin to level off to make way for arable land, areas of thicker vegetation, villages and temples. Here small figures plough the land, picnic together or sail to unknown destinations.

Here in the low-lying land the forces of yin may be stronger, gathered in a quiet pool or a field. And it is here that the human element comes into play, integrating into this natural order and making use of the natural resources. The temples and houses are built of stone, wood or sun-baked clay, and the fields irrigated by the water flowing from the mountain. The land in the picture, whether it is farmed or high on a mountain slope, is a reflection of the earth, and so the complete painting creates a harmonious relationship between heaven, earth and humanity.

While the idyllic scene described above may still be found in some rural areas of China, the demands of an increasing population put pressure upon the land and its resources. In order to meet these demands there may not be the time or the money to consider whether a town has been built too close to a swift-flowing river or too far from the protective influence of a mountain. However, feng shui does continue to be practised on a small scale, particularly when siting and laying out a building.

FENG SHUI AND THE LAND

Every natural site and every building is said in feng shui to be surrounded by four animal spirits, one each to the back and front, and to the right and left (see opposite).

The black tortoise protects the site so it should be higher than the red bird. The white tiger and the green dragon are guardians, and should be higher than the red bird but lower than the black tortoise. If this is translated into features in the landscape, a site should be sheltered by a hill at the back, preferably south-facing, and the slope should be gentle so ch'i can flow down to the site at an even pace. The site itself should be built on the slopes of the black tortoise with raised land to the sides and the front for protection.

In relation to a building the four animal spirits guard each side of it as shown opposite below.

The land behind the house should be flat if the garden is

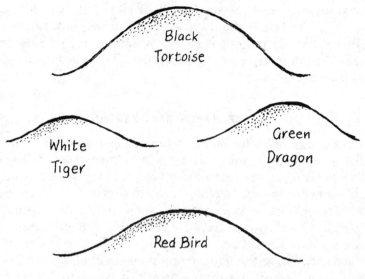

A classic feng shui site in the landscape

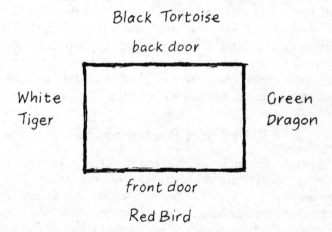

The four animals spirits guarding each side of a building

small or sloping slightly towards the house if the garden is
large. If the land behind slopes down from the house, ch'i
could slip away so it would be best to plant a screen of trees

or shrubs to slow the movement of ch'i. The land to the front of the house should also be flat or slightly sloping. Once again, if the slope is too steep leading from the house or to the house, the positive effects of ch'i may be lost unless its flow is controlled.

Using Trees and Plants

Trees and plants with their yin/yang properties have a valuable role in feng shui practice. Not only can they be used effectively to channel the flow of ch'i, but they are also valuable sources of ch'i. Greenery activates fresh ch'i and helps disperse malign or stagnant forces that may have accumulated in a lifeless area. Trees are particularly effective but, of course, they should not be planted too close to the house since they block the light, undermine the foundations and may be a hazard in a thunderstorm. It is not necessary to plant in every available spot; in feng shui one well-placed tree can often be more effective than a grove of trees.

All species of trees and shrubs can be beneficial to the feng shui of a house, although evergreens, which are a strong source of yang, are particularly auspicious. However, the harmony that vegetation creates is adversely affected by dead wood or disease in the plant and this should be removed or treated as soon as possible.

Water as a Source of Ch'i

Water, a fundamental yin force, is also a strong source of ch'i, although the benefit that is drawn from it is affected by its flow, position and purity. A river or stream that meanders at an even pace creates beneficial ch'i for those who live among the curves of its course and it is said that they are protected by a 'jade belt'. Fast, flowing water and sharp twists or bends in a watercourse can disperse ch'i too quickly and stagnant or polluted water can spread disease. When the flow of ch'i is limited it can decay or disappear to be replaced by sha (life-taking breaths). The positive elements are then overcome by negative elements, and sickness, financial loss, family disputes or other setbacks may follow. Sha can be found in drains, swampy or stagnant water, in dumping grounds, in refuse, or in dark, lifeless areas.

Sha also appears in cold, piercing winds that cut through gaps or hollows. Sha can also spread a malign influence by travelling along natural or human-made straight lines such as railway lines, roads or canals, so the corners of buildings or gardens that face on to them should be protected by fencing or vegetation. Fresh water in a garden pond or swimming pool can also help to disperse sha as long as the water is kept free of decaying vegetable matter or pollutant.

The branches, turns and twists of a watercourse are known as the water dragon and guidance for the siting of house in relation to a watercourse is contained in a Chinese text known as the *Water Dragon Classic*. Some of the feng shui interpretations contained in this work are shown below.

FENG SHUI AND THE DESIGN OF YOUR HOUSE

Outside the House

Although there is a wealth of practical advice about applying feng shui, its application also contains a strong element of personal common sense and taste. Colours, shapes or designs that suit one person may be difficult to live with for another, and sometimes all it takes to create a sense of harmony is a change of colour, a move of furniture or the introduction of a plant or a light. Here an understanding of whether you are a predominantly yin or yang household also counts.

Listed below you will find the basic feng shui principles for interior and exterior design.

- When you are looking at a house or apartment the build-ing should convey an overall sense of balance. It doesn't

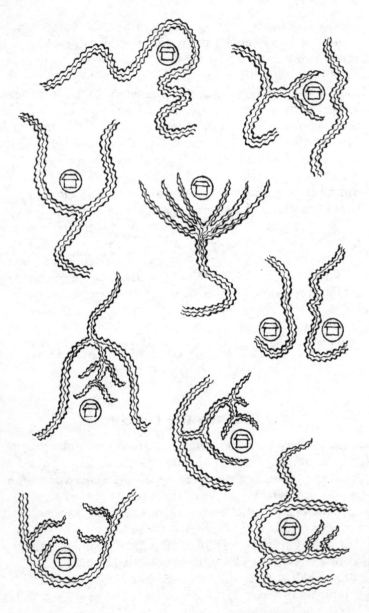

Favourable sites for a building in relation to a watercourse

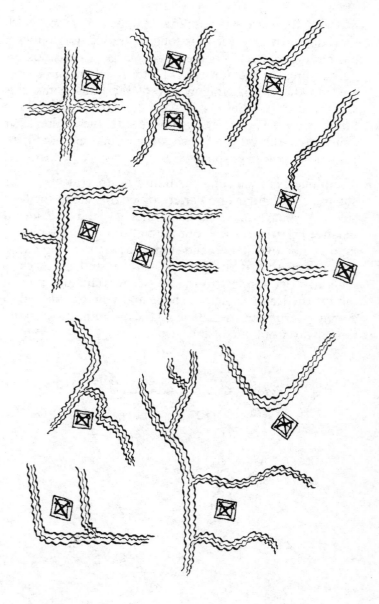

Unfavourable sites for a building in relation to a watercourse

matter if there are bay windows, extensions, more width than depth or vice versa as long as the design creates a harmonious effect. If there are large extensions or outbuildings to the house it is better for them to be situated on the Green Dragon side of the house since this animal spirit is believed to have a quiet nature. But if the house is top heavy on the opposite side, the White Tiger gains strength and the Green Dragon may be unable to control its powerful spirit.

- The plot of land around the house or apartment can be square, rectangular or a variety of lengths along the four sides. A square or rectangular plot of land provides a balanced setting for the four animal spirits. If the plot of land is narrow at one end and wide at the other it is better feng shui if the front is narrow and the back is wide to offer support to the house. A triangular plot of land is the least auspicious shape and you are advised to soften one of the triangular edges by adding or taking land away from one of the corners.

A triangular plot of land is
considered unlucky feng shui

- Try to avoid buildings that are close to stagnant water, waste disposal sites, low-lying land or exposed high land since they may be subject to sha. If this is unavoidable you can raise the level of the land, aerate the soil, introduce fresh water or plant trees to encourage fresh ch'i into the area. Mirrors are also highly regarded in feng shui since they are believed to reflect back malign forces and protect those living in a building. A mirror placed in the direction of an unlucky area will help to deflect forces which drain positive ch'i.

- Positive features around the house include a pond in front of the house (but not too close to the front door), a lamp or lamps outside the front door (which act as guardians) and a driveway which runs to the side of the house (to avoid ch'i disappearing out of the front door and straight down the drive).

A lamp by the front door acts as a guardian, while a driveway to the side helps conserve ch'i

- The house should not be dwarfed by buildings to each side or buildings to the front since this can interrupt the flow of ch'i over and around the house. Nor should houses, offices or shops be too tightly packed together, since this narrows the channels that ch'i can pass through. If there are higher buildings at a reasonable distance behind the house they can act as protection.

The house should not be dwarfed by buildings to the side and the front

- If you face on to a busy main road, try to erect a screen of trees or a fence so that money or good fortune is not drained from the house. Trees would also provide protection from fumes and noise, but make sure that they are planted more than 3ft from the house.

- Good fortune could be drawn away from a house, office or other building that sits on a sharp outside curve of a road, river or railway line. The sharp bend is likened to a knife or a scythe cutting into the property.

- A house at the end of a long straight road or facing the junction of two converging roads could be overwhelmed by the oncoming forces, and the health of those living there may be affected. A mirror or trees outside the house could help deflect these forces. If your house faces a gap between two buildings money could slip through your grasp.

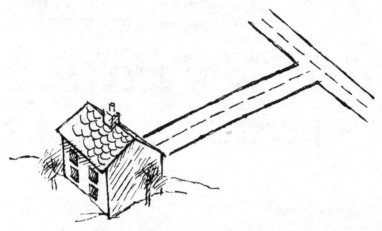

The forces travelling down straight roads could disturb the harmony of the house

Money could slip away through a gap facing your house

Inside the House

The main bedroom, living room and kitchen are the three most important rooms in the house for applying feng shui. The feng shui of the main bedroom is particularly relevant since the quality of sleep of its occupants can affect the health and relationships of everyone else in the house.

The feng shui of these three rooms and all the other rooms in the house are affected by the flow of ch'i. You should avoid crowding the rooms with furniture and objects since this hampers the smooth flow of ch'i. Try to bring light and greenery (yang) into dark, cramped corners (yin), and soften sharp corners to walls and corridors with plants.

The Bedroom

- In China the head of the bed is traditionally placed towards the east since this is the hottest (yang) side of the house and the practice has carried through into feng shui. The two least auspicious areas to place the bed are behind the door because you have no control over who enters the room, or directly facing the door since this could drain your energy. If the bed is in either of these positions you could break the access with a piece of furniture or plants and hang a mirror opposite the door to deflect unlucky influences. Do not place a mirror directly opposite the head of the bed in case you wake up unexpectedly and are frightened by your reflection!

- Exposed beams or rafters above the bed are believed to cause various minor illnesses as well as obstruct the smooth flow of ch'i through the bedroom. A beam over the head of the bed is said to cause headaches and nervous disorders, over the middle of the bed it may cause stomach disorders, and over the foot of the bed it

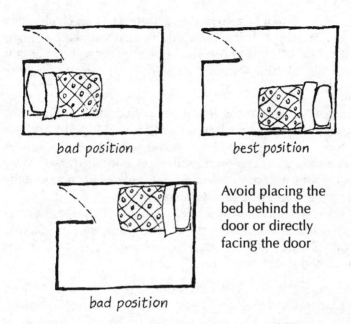

bad position   best position

Avoid placing the
bed behind the
door or directly
facing the door

bad position

could result in swollen feet. Two ways to remedy the situation are a false ceiling, or a mirror on the beam or rafter.

- Use soft colours and gentle lighting to create a relaxing mood and avoid very bright lights, particularly over the bed, since they are thought to cause liver problems. If you do have wall lights above the bed keep them dimmed and if one of the bulbs fails, replace it immediately.

- The bedroom should not face directly on to the kitchen or lavatory since the smells or steam could disturb your sleep. If they are close to each other they should be separated by a door or partition.

The Living Room

- There should be easy access from the front door to the living room, although the front door should not open directly on to a large living room since too much ch'i may enter or escape. If it is unavoidable that you walk straight into a large living room you should put a screen, a plant or a piece of furniture near the door to control the flow of ch'i.

- As you walk into the living room there is a point in the top left-hand corner known as the wealth point and the good fortune that collects here should be protected. A door or arch at this point will allow good fortune to flow away and a kettle placed here could result in the lucky forces evaporating in the steam.

  You are advised to place a plant with large, healthy green leaves just below the wealth point and to increase your chances of prosperity you should place three coins wrapped in red paper under the pot.

- Plants, light or water activate ch'i in the room and an aquarium is also a useful addition to help invigorate ch'i. You are advised to keep an odd number of goldfish in your aquarium since water is yin and odd numbers are yang, so harmony is created between the two, and further luck is added because the colour gold is associated with wealth.

The Kitchen

- The kitchen is said to be the 'treasure' of the house since it is the room where family and friends are catered and cared for. Ideally, the kitchen door should not face directly on to the front or back door of the house since the positive ch'i within the house may escape too quickly. Neither should a kitchen door directly face a lavatory door since germs could spread easily.

- The cooker, obviously yang, is regarded as the focal point of the kitchen and it should not be next to the sink or the fridge (both yin forces) unless there is a piece of panelling separating the two; this is based on the principle that the element of fire is destroyed by the element of water. The cooker should also be placed away from the window or from direct sunlight to prevent food deteriorating with exposure to the sun.

FENG SHUI AT WORK

- Since business is dependent upon customers the entrance to an office should be wider than that of a domestic building. The level of the entrance should also be slightly higher than the street outside, and it should be kept clean and brightly painted to encourage customers and good business ch'i to enter.

- The front of the building should not face the corners of buildings or narrow gaps between two buildings. Sharp corners may slice into the business and narrow gaps could drain money away.

A shop or office should not face a gap between two buildings
or the sharp corner of another building

- Once inside the office or shop, workers or customers should walk into a bright, open space which creates a positive feeling. If the first impression you have is of cramped, dark conditions the sense of pressure it creates may carry forward into business negotiations.

- The front door should not open directly on to a flight of stairs since the positive ch'i that is circulating the building could easily be mischannelled and disappear out of the front door.

Ch'i, circulating through the building could disappear if the front door opens directly on to the staircase

- Unless the business demands that the manager or director is in the public eye, the office of the person in charge should be in a quiet place, and access to it should be wide and bright so ch'i does not become trapped or hindered.

- You are advised not to sit at a desk with your back to the door since you cannot see who enters the room, but if this is unavoidable place a mirror above the desk so you get a view of the door. Ideally you should be seated with your back to the wall so that you have support behind you and have a clear view of who enters or leaves the

room. Your best position is in the diagonal corner opposite the door so that the incoming ch'i is not
overwhelming.

These are basic feng shui guidelines which may be useful
when you are assessing the design of your home or workplace. Many unlucky situations can be remedied by
introducing plants, flowers, mirrors or different colours,
and sometimes all it takes to improve the feeling of a room
is a change or a shift of furniture. It is important to estab-
lish a sense of harmony and balance that suits you, so use
your own personal judgment, sensitivity and common sense
as well. This way you can help the yin/yang balance of
nature even if it is only in the confines of your own home
and workplace.

4

The Flow of Ch'i: Energy, Sexuality, Food and Health

HARMONY AND BALANCE in the body are central to Chinese notions of health and well-being. Something of this is captured in the English word 'disease' which means no longer to be at ease, in balance, in harmony: dis-ease. The belief that medicine and doctors were there to maintain the balance of the body and the harmony of the soul is encapsulated in the Chinese tradition that you pay the doctor while you are well and stop paying when the doctor has to treat you for sickness! A doctor's responsibility is to make sure you are not ill, not to just cure you when you do fall ill. The traditional role of doctors is to keep you well balanced so you don't fall ill.

The heart of Chinese attitudes to the well-being of the body is spelt out in *The Yellow Emperor's Classic of Internal Medicine*:

> *The Yellow Emperor said: 'The principle of Yin and Yang is the basic principle of the entire universe. It is the principle of everything in creation ... In order to treat and cure diseases one must search into their origin.*
>
> *Yang stands for peace and serenity. Yin stands for recklessness and turmoil. Yang stands for destruction and Yin stands for conservation. Yang causes evaporation and Yin gives shape to things ...*
>
> *Through these interactions of their functions, Yin and Yang, the negative and positive principles in nature, are responsible for diseases which befall those who are rebellious to the laws of nature as well as those who conform to them.*

The whole body is divided between yin and yang, and it is the vital interaction and indeed even competition between these two forces that keeps a body healthy and fit. Too much of one means imbalance and thus dis-ease. As *The Yellow Emperor's Classic* says:

> *The emotions of joy and anger are injurious to the spirit. Cold and heat are injurious to the body. Violent anger is hurtful to Yin, violent joy is hurtful to Yang. When rebellious emotions rise to Heaven, the pulse expires and leaves the body.*

The heat of joy fuels the yang – hot – aspect of ourselves and thus means the balance with the yin – cool – aspect of us is threatened. This expresses itself in fevers and hot flushes. The chill of anger fuels the yin aspect of us, thus tipping the balance against the yang, hot aspect of us. This expresses itself in chills and colds.

Once you adopt a yin and yang model of the body, you can begin to read illnesses in terms of their relationship to these opposing forces. The whole thrust of traditional Chinese medicine is to maintain the balance and to compensate when one force – yin or yang – gets out of hand and threatens the harmony of the body.

In traditional Chinese thought, each part of the body is related to either yin or yang, and is also related to the five elements of wood, fire, earth, metal and water.

Yang Parts of the Body

Liver	ears	stomach
heart	nose	ligaments
spleen	gall bladder	arteries
eyes	small intestine	muscles

The back part of the body, the upper part of the body and the outer parts of the body are also related to yang.

Yin Parts of the Body

Lungs	penis	skin
kidneys	vagina	hair
mouth	large intestine	bones
anus	bladder	

The front part of the body, the lower part of the body and the inner organs generally (with the exception of those listed under yang) are also related to yin.

These can be further broken down under the five elements, three of which, wood, fire and earth, belong to yang, leaving metal and water to yin. Thus we find that under the yang categories of the body, the liver, eyes, gall bladder and ligaments are of the element wood; the heart, ears, small intestine and arteries are of the element fire; while the spleen, nose, stomach and muscles are of the element earth.

Those parts of the body under the yin category break down as follows. The lungs, mouth, large intestine, skin and hair are of the element metal; the kidneys, lower orifices, bladder and bones are of the element water.

	WOOD	FIRE	EARTH	METAL	WATER
YANG	liver eyes gall bladder ligaments	heart ears small intestine arteries	spleen nose stomach muscles		
YIN				lungs mouth large intestine skin hair	kidneys lower orifices bladder bones

These classifications are important because of the relationships between the five elements. As we saw in chapter 1, the elements can both create and destroy. In seeking to heal or mend the body, it is vital to know which element is uppermost and whether yin or yang is dominant in that part of the body which is affected, and whether yin or yang can assist its cure or healing. If it is, for example, the heart which needs strengthening then there is no point giving herbal medicine which stokes up the yin aspect or which fuels the power of water, for the yin will overwhelm the yang of the heart making it too cool, while the water element will put out the fire element. Thus the ability of the heart to pump warming blood throughout the body will be decreased and the illness will get worse.

In a nutshell, the basis of Chinese medicine and of Chinese concepts of health is balance and harmony. This provides perhaps the greatest single example of how the yin/yang theory works out in practice. Even with the advent of western scientific and medical skills and knowledge, medicine in China today still operates upon this model of how the body is constituted and of the need to maintain balance. Indeed, when the Communist government took power in China in 1949 they determined that Chinese medicine should walk on two legs – western medicine and traditional medicine – and it still does to this day.

EXCESSES OF YIN OR YANG

The outward manifestations of an excess of yin or yang are quite straightforwardly outlined by Chinese medicinal texts. For example excess yin manifests itself in a tendency to condense, in the skin having a purple hue, in a cold temperature, in weight gain, in excess water, in darkness of skin and in nervousness. An excess of yang manifests itself through a tendency to develop or grow, in red colour, in hotness, in loss of weight, in bright or shiny skin and in excessive activity.

To have a healthy body you need to be constantly in flux between yin and yang. No one is one or the other. We are a constantly altering state of yin moving to yang and yang moving to yin. Change is central to an understanding of health. Thus any attempt to take hold of a given state or being or appearance is to go against the flow of Tao and working of nature which exists through change – as we saw in chapter 2.

These are the signs of too much yin:

APPEARANCE quiet • withdrawn • sluggish • vulnerable • weary • lacking in drive • tongue moist, pale and slightly swollen.

ATTRIBUTES   voice is weak • breathing shallow with shortness of breath • breath smells acrid.

SYMPTOMS   feels cold • little appetite • urinates a lot and passes clear urine.

PULSE   thin and frail.

These are the signs of too much yang:

APPEARANCE   agitated • active and restless • quick in movement • tongue is red and dry.

ATTRIBUTES   voice is rough and loud, and patient wants to talk • deep breathing and breath smells putrid.

SYMPTOMS   feels hot • is constipated • passes dark urine and has a dry mouth.

PULSE   rapid and strong.

(Adapted from Ted Kaptchuk's *Chinese Medicine*,
see Bibliography)

CH'I: THE VITAL YANG ENERGY

While the human body is a conglomerate of the two forces of yin and yang and the five elements, it is animated by ch'i. Ch'i is breath and it is ch'i which brings life to the physical aspects. According to Taoist belief, when you are conceived you receive all the ch'i – breath – that you will ever have. This ch'i is what keeps you alive, so any loss of ch'i is loss of years of life. This is why Taoist initiates seeking long life avoid foods which produce wind! Any loss of breath other than through the normal process of breathing out is to be regretted and limits the span of life.

Ch'i is the original breath of existence. It is seen in many writings as being either equal to the Tao or as being its main manifestation. It is what condenses into the yin and evaporates into the yang. It is what moves within all life and without it life ceases. The *Pao Pu Tzu*, one of the most important Taoist texts, dating from the 4th century AD and written by the great Taoist philosopher and doctor Pao Pu, spells it out:

> *We exist in the chi and the chi resides inside us. From Heaven and Earth down to all living beings, there is no one nor any thing that does not need chi for life to continue. One who knows how to ensure the circulation of chi preserves integrity and banishes the evil forces which bring harm.*

Chuang Tzu relates this universal breath to the breath that animates the human being:

> *Life follows death and death is the forerunner of life. Who can know their ways?*
> *Human life begins with the original breath;*
> *When it comes together there is life,*
> *When it is dispersed, there is death.*
>
> *As death and life are together in all this, which should be termed bad? All the forms of life are one, yet we regard some as beautiful because they are spiritual and wonderful; others we count as ugly because they are diseased and rotting. But the diseased and rotting can become the spiritual and wonderful, and the spiritual and wonderful can become the diseased and rotting.*
>
> *It is said, 'All that is under Heaven is one breath.' The sages always comprehend such unity.*

Within the body, which being material is fundamentally yin, the ch'i is the yang energy which, together with the yin of the physical body, establishes the basic balance and harmony of existence. Well-being is ensured by easy circulation of the ch'i throughout the body. Taking imagery from the *Tao Te Ching* relating to the water-like nature of the Tao, Taoists have developed a vast array of meditational practices which concentrate on visualising the free flowing of ch'i throughout the body. Any sense of the ch'i being blocked is taken as a sign that there are physical or psychophysical problems in that part of the body.

The necessity of allowing the ch'i to move freely throughout the body is that it has to interact with the essence of the yin aspect of the body known as ching. The ching consists of consolidations of matter, so blood, saliva, sweat and semen are elements of the ching. The yin of the ching and the yang of the ch'i operate together to fuel, fire and drive the body. The balancing of the ch'i and ching is crucial to well-being. The Taoist Canon contains many books stressing the inter-relationship between the ch'i and the ching and the exercises necessary for well-being. For example, *Ku chi huan shen chiu chuan chiung tan lun*, 'The Study of the Path for Affirming the Breath and Causing the Soul to Return', says:

> to strengthen the ching, one must first perfect the chi; to strengthen the chi, one must first make the ching return. Thus if the chi is perfect, the yang ching does not decrease: if the ching returns the original chi is not dispersed.

One of the key texts of this approach to the body is the *Book of the Yellow Court*, Huang Ting Ching, which dates from around the 3rd century AD. Combining the universe in the body concept we explored in chapter 2 with the balancing of the body, it envisages the spirit world as existing within your own body. Through meditation upon the aspects of creation, diverse gods and goddesses within and their places of residence, you can come to understand or know the ways of your body and ensure the free flow of chi. For example, the creedal statement of Taoism is contained in chapter 42 of the *Tao Te Ching*. It reads as follows:

The Tao
gives birth to the One:
The One
gives birth to the Two;
the Two
gives birth to the Three –
The Three gives birth to every living thing.
All things are held in yin and carry yang:
And they are held together in the ch'i of teeming energy.

A classic Taoist meditation is to work your way up from the bottom. Start with ch'i. Sense it in yourself. Focus on it. Now follow it through your body – yin and yang – see lists on pages 62–3.

Next, you need the Three. This means Heaven, Earth and you. So feel your rootedness to the ground then reach up through your head to Heaven. Feet – Earth; Head – Heaven. Next go to the Two – yin and yang. Feel yin in your bowels and yang in your blood.

Then go to the One – unity – you and the cosmos; you and all deities are One. Finally release yourself into Tao – the way of Nature. There is no distinct 'you' now. 'You' are part of everything.

This meditation takes years to perfect so don't expect miracles. Just put aside time regularly to work on it.

Exercises designed to move the ch'i around the body follow highly structured programmes and formed, indeed still do form, the focal point of the Taoist meditational practices performed on remote mountain tops or in city monasteries. One of the major exponents of this approach to the body was the 8th century AD writer Ssu Ma Cheng Cheng, who set out a classic method or programme of using the ch'i to energise the five elements and the five viscera of the body:

In spring, on the six ping days at 9.00–11.00 a.m. eat
the breath [draw your breath and energy back into the
body in a conscious act] 120 times and guide it to the

heart, in such a way that the heart outweighs the lungs, but without the lungs harming the liver. This is the breath which nourishes the liver.

In summer, on the six mu days at 1.00–3.00 p.m. eat the breath 120 times to help the spleen, so that the spleen outweighs the kidneys, but without the kidneys harming the heart.

In the third month of summer, on the six keng days at 3.00–5.00 p.m. eat the breath 120 times to help the lungs, so that the lungs outweigh the liver, but without the liver harming the spleen.

In autumn, on the six jen days at 9.00–11.00 p.m. eat the breath 120 times to help the kidneys, so that the kidneys outweigh the heart, but without the heart harming the lungs.

In winter, on the six chia days at 3.00–5.00 a.m. eat the breath 120 times to help the liver, so that the liver outweighs the spleen, but without the spleen harming the kidneys ... Each breath nourishes its internal organ; when it has gone its route, it is begun again; they must not harm one another. Perform it with care.

Exercising Your Yin and Yang

One of the most well-known methods of seeking a healthy body and balance is to follow a physical exercise routine such as Tai Chi Chuan. The essence of all the different systems is the same, namely, to ensure the free and easy flow of the vital ch'i energy to all parts of the body. This in turn helps to maintain a balance between the yin and yang forces within the body.

All the Taoist and Buddhist systems use the same model of which parts of the body need to be exercised and in what order. The core of this is that there are five fundamental sub-divisions of the body:

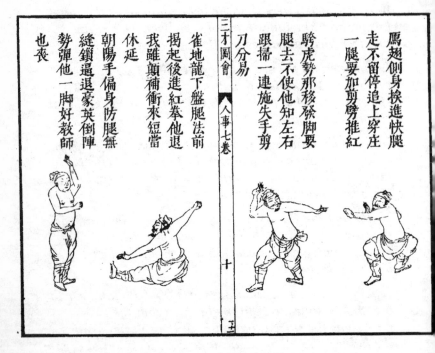

Traditional illustrations of Tai Chi Chuan movements

1. Internal

2. External

3. Front

4. Back

5. Central

This describes, first, the internal organs of the body which, by using visualisation, you move the ch'i energy through. The external attributes, such as skin, hair, etc., can be enlivened in just the same way. The flow of ch'i goes from front to back and its source, its centre, is the centre of the body. Thus, through a circular movement of the ch'i from internal to external, from front to back and returning to the centre, all parts of the body are reached.

A further five categories used are the parts of the body to be moved and exercised in order. The order runs as follows:

1. Head

2. Torso

3. Arms, hands and fingers

4. Legs, feet and toes

5. Return to centre.

By following this flow, the ch'i is moved in a cycle round the body.

Finally there are the five ways of moving the ch'i. These are:

1. Up and down

2. Forward and return

3. Sideways

4. Centrifugally

5. Centripetally.

These exercises are not just about physical well-being. They are also about maintaining a balance between mind, body and spirit – to use a western division of the person. You are not just your body, but also your mind, your experiences and your potential. Thus, these exercises are designed to bring the balancing flow of ch'i to your spirit, your mind, your body, your energy and your health. Only together can these offer you a true sense of well-being. As with everything to do with yin and yang, it is maintaining the harmony between diverse aspects of you that is important. Over-exercising the body can lead to as many problems as under-exercising. Balance is all in the yin and yang of health.

In the monasteries and sacred mountains of China, you can still meet masters who have developed these arts to such an extent that they seem to float rather than walk. For most Chinese, however, a half-hour in the park at sunrise or sunset, slowly moving through the physical and mental exercises with dignity, is enough.

Regulating Your Yin and Yang

Alongside these physical exercises there lies a tradition of balancing the body by detecting the imbalances manifested by extremes of hot or cold, by colour, by pulse and other external indicators of internal imbalance. Many Chinese will regulate themselves. They will long ago have decided whether they are predominantly a yin or yang personality. They will have learnt which parts of the body are predominantly yin or yang, and which element is associated with those parts of the body. They will probably do simple exer-

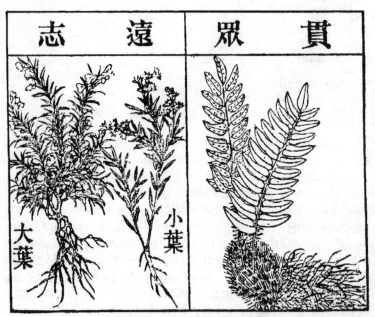

Herb illustrations from a traditional Chinese text

cises to ensure the free flow of the ch'i, and they will keep a check on temperature and other factors which can indicate a disturbance in the balanced harmony of their bodies. If the balance begins to show serious signs of being out of kilter, then the use of simple herbal remedies will often be sufficient to restore the balance.

Thus, for example, a classic result of a predominance or excess of yin is low blood pressure or general weariness. To counter this the yang needs to be stoked up. This can be done using yang herbs such as ginseng or wolfbane. In contrast, a classic result of a predominance of yang results in high blood pressure and constipation. To deal with this, a yin herb such as rhubarb is used.

As can clearly be seen, balance and harmony are the very purpose and methodology of Chinese health and medicine. Keeping the body tuned up, allowing neither an excess of yin nor yang, is fused with the recognition that the body is also always changing. Thus, the Chinese view of the body combines prevention with realism Those searching for eternal youth will never find it in Chinese belief. Ageing is a natural process. However, what you will find is the quest for immortality.

THE QUEST FOR BODILY IMMORTALITY

In Taoist belief, it is possible to become an immortal and thus to never die. But to do this you must preserve your physical body. This is very different from most other faiths which stress that the body is of relatively little significance spiritually and that it is the soul which passes on into eternity. In Chinese thought there is no immortality without a body to inhabit and that body has to be the one you have on earth.

This view of the body as being capable of eternity ties in with the vision of the body as the universe in microcosm, for if the ultimate nature of the body is that it is capable of being the Tao or of at least being at one with the flow of Tao, then the body is capable of being part of the eternal nature of the Tao. The body, in other words, is not just a husk or shell in which the immortal soul is trapped. It is actually part of the eternal reality of existence, part of the Tao, fed by the eternal ch'i, residence of yin and yang and constituted of the five elements.

The quest for immortality of the body has traditionally taken two forms in China. One, the external school, tried to replace the perishable flesh and bone with imperishable materials. They argued, perhaps to its logical conclusion, that 'you are what you eat'. Therefore they experimented with digesting materials which never perish – gold, jade and mercury being favourites. While it is true that these do not perish it is also true that they can quite easily poison! So, many of those searching for immortality passed painfully away at a young age, poisoned by the very elements they thought would ensure eternity!

The second approach is the internal school which sought to develop the body as a place wherein that which is life giving – namely the ch'i, yin and yang – would never perish, so the body would have no reason to die. If the original breath ch'i could be kept going for ever, then the body would grow older and older but would never die. If the yin and yang were kept fed and active, then, again, the body would grow old but not die. This is why almost all the famous immortals of Chinese belief are not young things, dwelling in perpetual youthfulness, or rejuvenated by the elixir of youth. They are old men and women, who have over the years developed their bodies to such a point that they have complete control over them and thus ensure the preservation of the ch'i, and the yin and yang.

However, there is also another version of this school, which saw the external body as being too fragile to sustain or survive such a quest. This school developed the idea of an embryo body which you nurture within you so that when the moment of death comes, the old body fails but within it, ready to achieve immortality, is a new body, which for years has been fed and developed as the embryo body which will take you into eternity. This is done by recycling the vital force of the yin element within you – semen – and fusing it with the yang ch'i to produce a new life within you. As will be immediately clear from the use of the word semen, this has been a practice developed by and for men. This reflects the inherent sexism of Chinese religion.

Through retention of the semen and by using exercises similar to those used for ch'i, to cycle the semen through the body, Taoism teaches that a new being can be created within you. This being – which is still you – grows as an embryo within you until your old body dies and the new body takes over. While many have taken this to be a literal description and perhaps been somewhat surprised at death to find there is no sign of this new body, others have taken it to have a spiritual meaning. Just as there was the earlier division between the external and internal schools, so the same division exists here. Today, few would claim they are growing a new body inside them. Most would see it as a spiritual metaphor for a life dedicated to self-perfection and virtue. However, this is an area of great mystery and not one which I have found many Taoists willing to discuss. Perhaps this is because so much of it is associated with sexual activity – and this tradition has been frowned upon and condemned by Taoist authorities for over a thousand years.

SEXUALITY: YIN AND YANG IN ACTION

It is perhaps time to look at the relationship between the sexes as understood through the yin yang model. After all, the division between male and female is a yang yin division.

Male and Female in the *I Ching*

At heart of the *I Ching* is an interaction between yin and yang. This is very clear from the first two hexagrams, Chien and Kun, for one is all yang and the other all yin. Put side by side like this they can be seen to complement each other (see p. 96). But in these two hexagrams we can begin to understand the relationship between male and female, and indeed begin to comprehend the traditional attitude to sexuality and to sex itself.

In the Appendices or Wings associated with the *I Ching* (in effect commentaries written around the 5th to 4th centuries BC and credited to Confucius), the male female aspects of hexagrams 1 and 2 are spelt out:

> *Vast is chien, the beginner. All things owe to it their beginning. It comprises Heaven ... The way of chien is to change and transform, so that everything obtains its proper nature according to its Fate ...*

> *Perfect is kun, the beginner. All things owe to it their birth. It receives obediently the influences of Heaven ...*

> *The way of chien constitutes the male; the way of kun constitutes the female. Chien knows the great beginning; kun gives to things their completion.*

The model arising from the *I Ching* is a classic one. It assumes the male yang principle is the active, begetting one, with the female yin principle being the docile, passive, receptive one. The male creates, the female just gives birth. This seems to have been a retrogressive model which arose from the Confucian influence upon the *I Ching*. It assumes a hierarchy of male over female, which is of course central to Confucian teachings. The Confucian filial piety order placed the male above the female, just as the emperor was above the subjects and the father above the son. The evidence which we can reconstruct about earliest Chinese society seems to point not to this classic sexist model but to a society in which men and women had effective equality. Certainly shamanic societies had male and female shamans, and each seems to have been as powerful and as accepted as the other.

Remnants of a More Equal Relationship Between Men and Women

The early mythology of China presents a world in which male and female were equal, and there is no evidence of a patriarchal society coming into existence until the Shang dynasty (c. 1500 BC). Even then, while political power became patriarchal, religious and spiritual power seems to have remained shared equally between men and women. However, by the end of the Shang, this was breaking down and there is a gradual shift to a conventional patriarchal society. By the time the Commentaries on the *I Ching* are written, the shift has been completed, and thus chien and kun are defined in standard sexist terms as the active male and the passive female.

Nor was it just the Confucians who adopted this position. The Taoists too developed a model of relationships which placed women in a very lowly position.

Despite this, Chinese writings, poetry, novels and erotic art spell out a different message. Alongside the traditional Confucian hierarchy model and the Taoist vision of women as evil traps which suck a man's vital powers and prevent him achieving immortality, there is a whole approach to male female relationships which takes the yin and yang as equals in a dynamic dance of relationship.

A casual glance at much Chinese art reveals that it is full of male/female symbolism. In traditional Taoist thought it was believed that when sexually stimulated, men and women secrete their essence – yin for women and yang for men. The creation of a new life through sexual intercourse was seen as being the creation of the cosmos in miniature by the interaction of the yin and yang essences. So sexual intercourse was a cosmic act – not so much a case of did the earth move but did the universe!

Chinese art is full of reference to sexuality, if you know the allusions. For example, a red bird, a piece of jade or coral, a dragon's head extended, a turtle's head protruding or a mushroom are symbols of the penis. A peach, a flowering peony blossom, a pink shell, a golden lotus or a vase are all symbols of the vagina. Great rainstorms, lightning and thunder, hunting birds swooping down on prey, plum blossom, birds pecking at grain, a carp struggling against a fish hook and a stem of a plant in a vase are all symbols of sexual intercourse. Once you begin to realise the extent of the sexual symbolism in Chinese art you soon appreciate that the yin yang of male female relationships pervades art. And it does so in a way which puts forward a more positive equality of the nature of this relationship than does either strict Confucianism or ascetic Taoism or Buddhism. It depicts a world of mutual interaction and enjoyment.

Sex as the Overcoming of the Yang

Officially, Confucianism taught that sexual intercourse was only valid for procreation. No pleasure should be taken in the act, nor should men waste their time with women except to ensure that they had sons to follow them and to offer the appropriate sacrifices. This is pressed home in the moralising narratives of the Confucian historians. The fundamental belief of Confucians was that male energy, both physical and intellectual, is dissipated by sexual union over and above that necessary for procreation. The result of excessive sexual intercourse on men is to turn them into exhausted and morally worn out specimens. The state of the women is of no concern to the Confucians.

While such a state of exhaustion was bad enough in ordinary men, in the emperor it was tantamount to losing the right to rule. In the conventional histories of the dynasties, the moral decline and sexual excesses of the last ruler or two of each dynasty was a prerequisite. It explained why the dynasty had lost the right and power to rule.

So, at one level, the official code saw male female relationships in a purely male orientated family sense. In Taoism, this goes one step further. In certain schools of Taoism, there arose the belief that women, in the exchange of yin and yang essences in intercourse, drained a man of the yang force which kept him alive. Worse, the secretion of female yin essences into a man's body through absorption through the penis weakened his yang nature, leading to a diminished lifespan. However, it was also obvious that if the sexual act created yang essences in a man, this was in itself a good thing, for such essences, if retained in the man's body, might feed his yang nature and ensure a longer life. So a whole technique of seeking immortality for men developed which taught methods of sexual intercourse with women, where at the last moment the man held back his discharge of semen – the yang essences – and reabsorbed it into his own body. Indeed, this school of thought went on to say that a man should seek to couple with as many women as possible in a day or night, in order to create as much yang as possible, but never to discharge it.

It has to be said that this teaching was only ever followed by the more extreme Taoists – both lay and monastic. But it did influence sexual relationships more generally in that it became linked to the idea of creating and nurturing the embryo body within the physical body, as we saw earlier. If at the right moment the man could retain his semen, this would then help to give birth to this new body within and then feed it, ready for the embryo body to take over the role of the old physical body at death. It also led of course to the woman being viewed as nothing more than a stimulant for the man, or worse, to being a dangerous creature who might actually absorb your yang essences, thus denying you long life.

It has to be faced that much of the relationship between men and women in traditional Chinese society was oppressive and destructive to women. The balance and harmony sought by men was at the expense of women. It was a world view in which women were kept to their lowly and servile role; one in which their passivity and receptivity balanced the activity and energy of the male. It was a balance between the external world of men's affairs and the internal world of the home – the woman's realm. It is rather clearly signified by the Chinese character for peace – a woman under the hand of a man or under a roof.

Restoring the Balance Between Male and Female

In ridding ideas of yin and yang of the sexist overlaps of the sort of hierarchical model spelt out in the *I Ching's* ancient commentaries, we can perhaps return to a purer and more helpful relationship between the yin and the yang of relationships and of sexuality. Taking all that has been said earlier about the necessity of the one for the other, but also all that has been said about the nature of struggle, diversity and difference which each has, perhaps we can learn something about the nature of relationships between men and women. Much of recent writing on the need for men to discover and explore the feminine aspects of themselves has a ring of the insights of yin and yang, the necessity of balance and harmony where conflicting or divergent forces are present.

The yin yang model offers a way of recognising the potential for conflict and for recognising the inherent difference, while at the same time acknowledging the need of the one for the other. In the modern world, many look for peace or harmony as an end to struggle and difference. It always eludes us, for it cannot exist by itself. In relationships, the constant give and take of personal and sexual aspects of being in a relationship means that unless we have a model which handles such interaction positively, we will react negatively.

As has been pointed out before, a man can be predominantly yin and a woman predominantly yang. What is clear from the yin yang model is that there will always be one who is more active, more assertive than the other. The complementarity of yin and yang is about the complementarity of difference. Again, we have tended to see difference as traditionally meaning division. But yin and yang show us that it is not division. It is diversity.

In recognising that as a man, I might be more yin than yang, I can be freed from some feeling of male inadequacy, and can enjoy and develop this aspect of who I am. Likewise, by looking at my relationships with others in terms of whether their yin or yang nature complements and differs from my own balance, I have a way of assessing relationships which transcends the normal terms used in the West. Using the yin yang model can be a real liberation.

We live in a culture which favours the yang aspect in preference to the quieter yin aspect. Our contemporary world is a yang, masculine world. We need to be reminded that to go too far that way is to court disaster. The rising of the yin is inevitable and, for many, long sought and much hoped for. In time, this will go too far and the pendulum will swing back again. But for us living now, these are exciting times, for the zenith of the yang phase has passed and we are now heading, I would argue, inexorably towards the rising of the yin. The world is going to be a very different sort of place as a result.

In working slowly and at times painfully towards a more equal society, we have little to learn from traditional, hierarchical, sexist Chinese lifestyles. But we have much to learn from the concept of yin and yang, male and female being locked together in struggle and in difference, and yet being within each other as well. It is this dynamic, active model of relationships which can help to indicate a way forward which does not deny either the male or the female, the yang or the yin, but sees them as capable of complementarity through difference.

THE FOOD OF THE GODS

Any one who knows China and the Chinese will be aware how important cooking is to them! It is therefore no surprise to discover that the same concept of balance as revealed by the Tao is found in the theories and practice of Chinese cooking. The *Tso Chuan*, a commentary of the 3rd century BC, contains the following insight:

> *Harmony may be illustrated by soup. You have the water and fire, vinegar, pickle, salt and plums, with which to cook fish. It is made to boil by the firewood and the cook mixes the ingredients, harmoniously equalizing the several flavours so as to supply whatever is deficient and carry off whatever is in excess. Then the master eats it and his mind is made equable.*

Just as there are the five notes in music (see chapter 5) and the five elements of wood, fire, earth, metal and water, so there are the five tastes. These five tastes are salt, sweet, sour, hot and pungent. All five are supposed to be present in any dish, and they must always balance and harmonise. Throughout a meal, the five tastes may each predominate within one or more dishes, but overall the meal must balance out. The five tastes are further supplemented by the five textures – namely dryness, smoothness, crispness, juiciness and softness. Again, each dish should contain these five and the whole meal be a balance between them. The five colours of green, red, yellow, white and black are also supposed to be present at each meal.

By carefully combining the different elements and thus by reflecting the yin/yang dynamic, food becomes a means of sustaining the Tao. It is also vital to sustaining the physical body as the microcosm of the universe. Given the Taoist stress on the need to preserve your physical body in order to ensure immortality, food came to have spiritual significance in a very material way! I have already commented upon the fact that those wishing to preserve their original breath, their ch'i, refrain from eating things that produce wind – garlic, onions and so forth. To this was added a desire to eat those things thought to symbolise long life, such as mushrooms, turtle and deer – all thought to live for many centuries – and the delight in peaches for their sexuality (they represent the vagina) and their role in longevity.

But food also stokes the yin and yang in other ways, by adding to the heating of the body or the cooling of the body. The notion of hot or cold in relation to the body does not refer to whether the food tastes hot or is served cold, or only in a very minor way. What is important is the inherent yang or yin quality of the food itself. Thus rich, high-calorie, spicy foods are seen to bring extra heat into the body, and this may cause fevers, constipation, rashes and so forth. Conversely, low calorie, white, black or green coloured foods (these are seen as cool colours) can introduce coolness into the body. Vegetables, particularly vegetables of the right colour like green or white radishes or watercress, are seen as cool foods. Eat too much of them and you may end up with general weakness, shivering, colds and sallow coloured skin.

Added to this is whether a food is dry or wet. This again reflects the yin/yang theory and again is seen as essential to health. By balancing dry foods against wet foods, you can correct any excessive dryness of the body or excessive dampness of the body. The 7th century AD physician Sun Ssu Mo summed up the relationship between food and health very succinctly:

> *A truly good physician first finds out the cause of the illness. Having found that out, he first tries to cure it by food. Only when food has failed does he prescribe medicine.*

In understanding Chinese food in yin and yang terms, remember that you the eater bring a yin or yang element to the table. All foods have therefore to be evaluated with regard to the particular balance of the one who eats it. Nevertheless, certain basic balances of food can still be sought.

You probably know this from your own experience. There are certain foods which, when you are in a particular mood, you cannot eat without ill effects. I cannot drink coffee unless I am feeling well balanced. To do so when I am out of balance with myself or the world around is to run the risk of feeling very strange and ill at ease.

Your Own Yin and Yang Food Chart

Before you even try to work out a Chinese yin and yang diet, simply reflect on those foods which you are able to eat at any time; those which you use as a pick-me-up, probably when your yang energy is low; and those foods which you use as a relaxant – yin foods in essence. Finally, which foods can you not eat at certain times and would you describe them as yin or yang foods? By doing this you can begin to build up a yin/yang food chart of your own. Then you can start to look at the standard Chinese definitions.

All foods fall into three categories: yin foods; yang foods; neutral foods. The terms yin and yang relate to whether a food is a cooling food or a heating food. But do not be fooled by simple assumptions. These terms often have nothing whatsoever to do with the taste of a food, nor how it is cooked. They relate to deeper essences of the nature of a certain food. Thus one might assume that all drinks are cooling, but in fact beer is, while brandy is not. Here is a very basic list of yin, yang and neutral foods.

Yin Foods

Almonds • apple • asparagus • bamboo • banana • barley • beancurd • beansprouts • beer • broccoli • cabbage • celery • clams • corn • cornflour • crab • cucumber • duck • eels • fish • grapes • honey • ice-cream • lemons • mushrooms • mussels • oranges • oysters • peppermint tea • pineapple • salt • shrimps • spinach • strawberries • soyabeans • white sugar • tomatoes • water.

Yang Foods

Beef · black pepper · brown sugar · butter · cheese · chicken liver and fat · chillies · chocolate · coffee · curry · eggs · smoked fish · garlic · green peppers · goose · ham · kidney beans · lamb · leeks · onions · peanut butter · roasted peanuts · potato · rabbit · turkey · walnuts · whisky · wine.

Neutral Foods

Bread · carrots · cauliflower · cherries · lean chicken meat · dates · milk · peaches · peas · pigeon · plums · raisins · brown rice · steamed white rice.

Balancing Your Cooking

In planning a meal, you should pay attention to the type of people you are feeding and seek to balance the meal accordingly. Chinese dining is in essence a fine balance between a yang style of cooking and a yin style of drinking. Very few Chinese drink alcohol with their meal. This is for one simple reason. All Chinese food is cooked at very high temperatures in hot oil or fat. This means the method of cooking and the cooking material is yang – high energy and very fattening! To counter-balance this, you drink tea. Tea is usually yin and it acts as a dissolvant on the oil and fat. It clears the arteries and cools down the high energy level of the cooked food. So, serve alcohol if you want, but always serve a Chinese tea or your guests will become over-charged with the very yang nature of the meal.

A Chinese dish almost always combines at least two elements. For example, serve beef with nuts – yang and yin; pork with bamboo, again yang with yin. These combinations are designed to assist a predominantly yang dish to have a yin aspect. Throughout the meal, different dishes will be more yin or more yang than each other. This does not matter. What matters is the overall balance.

But don't think that you have to get it right every time! Chinese food is a long-term venture. Over a month or so, an overall balance needs to be maintained – but the season also affects what you need. In the winter, with yang at its lowest ebb, the Chinese have always gone for more yang foods such as dog or snake meat. In the summer, with yin at its lowest ebb, yin foods are served, fruits and nuts for example. The seasons, in what they provide for you to eat, are in themselves major indicators of whether a food is yin or yang. Winter foods are usually yang, while summer fruits and vegetables are on the whole yin. This is why eating seasonally has always been so important to the Chinese – indeed to all old peasant cultures. In a world where we can find strawberries in winter and peaches all the year round, we are in danger of putting our physical clocks out of synchronicity with the natural world of the seasons. And remember, the seasons are one of the major expressions of yin and yang in action.

5

Painting the Dragon: The Arts and Yin and Yang

ENACTING YIN AND YANG IN ART

THROUGHOUT CHINESE ART runs the motif of balancing diversity and of holding in creative tension that which is different. Chinese artists have also sought to show that yin and yang interact at all times, and thus create not stability and staidness, but action and change. The influence of the *I Ching* on Chinese art is enormous. Many text books on art use the yin and yang of the hexagrams of the *I Ching* to describe various emotions or states which art then seeks to represent or encapsulate. But perhaps the most important thing to appreciate about Chinese art is that there is no observer. Because the fundamental truth of art is that it holds in tension the yin and yang, then you the 'viewer' are in fact a part of the reality. You are a piece of the whole, an eddy in the flow of the Tao of which the painting or sculpture or artefact is also a part.

Landscape painting, probably one of the highest forms of art in China, is known as mountain and water art. As we saw in chapter 3, the mountain stands for the yang and the water for the yin. Both are of course manifestations of the Tao which is the origin of all. Thus does the 4th–5th century AD painter Tsung Ping describe the purpose or genesis of landscape painting:

> *Having embraced Tao the sage responds harmoniously*
> *to things. Having purified his mind the worthy man*
> *enjoys forms. As to landscapes, they exist in material*
> *substance and soar into the realm of the spirit ... Now*
> *the sage by exercise of his spirit follows Tao as his*
> *standard, while the worthy man understands this.*
> *Mountains and rivers in their form pay homage to Tao,*
> *and the man of humanity delights in them. Do not the*
> *sage and mountain and rivers have much in common?*

The aim of a landscape painting is to bring together the two worlds of the shaman – as Tsung Ping mentioned – the material substance and the realm of the spirit. This explains the delight in the deep river gorge with soaring mountain crags, or the perilously hanging lone pine with the moon. There are always images of the material world in interaction with the vastness of space.

The Changing Landscape

Landscape also captures the essence of wu-wei – the 'being-ness' of nature which exists without having to do. There are the forms and shapes created by the flow of water, the weathering by wind, the scarring by frost and the cracking by sun. The notion of change taking place but of no action underlying the change is vital. Roots of an old tree pushing apart a rock and water wearing away a cliff are images of

A traditional Chinese landscape painting combining deep river gorge with soaring mountain crags

the permanence of change which, as we have seen in chapter 4, is at the heart of the *I Ching* and of the *Tao Te Ching*.

In the vast gardens of the Imperial Palace in Peking or in the Summer Palace north of the city, you will find enormous, weathered rocks, notable for the wind-worn shapes and holes which have been carved into them by the natural action of rain, wind and water. It is clear that these great rocks have been transported at great effort and expense in order to be erected within the gardens. These rocks, worn by millennia of submersion in swirling waters, were one of the most expensive items it was possible to buy in Imperial times.

They were seen to exemplify the interaction of yin and yang, and to be the classic expression of the changes which are wrought even on that which seems changeless. As an artistic device they often appear in landscape paintings, or as the background to scenes of human life or courtship. The worn stone, holed by the wear of water, carved by the wind, is the ultimate in natural art – art as created solely by the Tao itself. In holding together both substance and emptiness it represents the yin and yang, the material and the spiritual.

Space in Paintings

People often comment upon the space within Chinese paintings – the sparseness of the brushstrokes in a pen and ink sketch or the emptiness at the heart of a landscape, framed by the sharply delineated natural features of rocks, mountain or water. This interaction between is and is not, between the material and the spiritual, is outlined in the *Tao Te Ching*'s comments upon the art of making things (from chapter 11).

Thirty spokes on a cart-wheel

Go towards the hub that is the centre

– but look, there is nothing at the centre
and that is precisely why it works!

If you mould a cup you have to make a hollow:
it is the emptiness within it that makes it useful.

In a house or room it is the empty spaces
– the doors, the windows – that make it usable.

They all use what they are made of
to do what they do,

but without their nothingness they would be nothing.

Reading this, one can begin to appreciate the appeal and significance of the worn stone with its holes.

The significance of using mountains and vast panoramas is, of course, that to the casual observer they are timeless. Mountains are forever, or so it seems. Yet, year by year, bit by bit, they are worn away, changed, broken and recreated. This theme of restless change pervades Chinese art.

From Change to Harmony

The other all-pervading motif is that of the intermingling and the harmony and balance which comes from this. Chinese pottery is famous for its wonderful slips. These were developed in part in order to show the harmony of interaction between different colours. The swirling blending of different coloured slips – as found in particular on Celadon ware or Kuan pottery – exemplify the merging of difference and the creation of subtlety and harmony from diversity. The placing of objects which symbolise yin and yang, in juxtaposition to each other, is a fundamental aspect of Chinese art, be it in painting, sculpture or pottery. We have seen that the mountain and the water is one obvious example, but so are the dragon (yang) flying in the clouds (yin); square objects (yin and the earth) beside circular objects (yang and heaven); and sweet and sour dishes in cooking.

The relationship between the artist and his or her material is also viewed as a harmony of intentions. This is very much the case with carving. The artist seeks to listen to the stone, gem or wood and to be attuned to follow the natural curves and possibilities of the material. A famous illustration of this, going with the grain, flowing with the Tao, is given in *Chuang Tzu*:

Cook Ting was butchering an ox for Lord Wen Hui. Every movement of his hand, every shrug of his shoulder, every step of his feet, every thrust of his knee every sound of the sundering flesh and the swoosh of the descending knife, were all in perfect accord, like the Mulberry Grove Dance or the rhythm of the Ching-shou.[1]

'Ah, how excellent!' said Lord Wen Hui. 'How has your skill become so superb?'

Cook Ting put down his knife and said, 'What your servant loves best is the Tao, which is better than any art. When I started to cut up oxen, what I saw was just a complete ox. After three years, I had learnt not to see the ox as whole. Now I practise with my mind, not with my eyes. I ignore my sense and follow my spirit. I see the natural lines and my knife slides through the great hollows, follows the great cavities, using that which is already there to my advantage. Thus I miss the great sinews and even more so, the great bones. A good cook changes his knife annually, because he slices. An ordinary cook has to change his knife every month, because he hacks. Now this knife of mine I have been using for nineteen years, and it has cut thousands of oxen. However, its blade is as sharp as if it had just been sharpened. Between the joints there are spaces, and the blade of a knife has no real thickness. If you put what has no thickness into spaces such as these, there is plenty of room, certainly enough for the knife to work through. However, when I come to a difficult part and can see that it will be difficult, I take care and due regard. I look carefully and I move with caution. Then, very gently, I move the knife until there is a parting and the flesh falls apart like a lump of earth falling to the ground. I stand with the knife in my hand looking around and then, with an air of satisfaction, I wipe the knife and put it away.'

'Splendid!' said Lord Wen Hui. 'I have heard what Cook Ting has to say and from his words I have learned how to live life fully.'

---

[1] Two very ancient forms of music.

THE ARTIST

The interaction between the artist and the – to a Western mind – inanimate materials of stone, wood, gem or paper is one of partners in a process. It is not the artist who creates, but it is the Tao, working through the artist and through the natural essence of the materials, which is expressed in art. This is well expressed by the 11th century AD Confucian philosopher Chang Tsai:

> *Heaven is my father and earth my mother, and even such a small being as I finds an intimate place in their midst. Therefore, that which fills the universe I regard as my body and that which directs the universe I regard as my nature. All people are my brothers and sisters, and all things are my companions.*

The artist is of the same being as that which he or she paints, or carves, or moulds. From their difference comes the possibility of creativity. Thus is art at its heart an outward expression of the Tao.

In the 6th century AD, the painter Hsieh Ho tried to codify this in his 'Six Principles of Painting', contained in the preface to his work, *Ku Hua Pin Lu*, 'Ancient Painter's Classified Record'. His six principles are:

1. harmonise the spirit, create life's motion;

2. use the brush in a structured way;

3. paint with fidelity what the object is;

4. conform to the colours of what is;

5. place the elements in balanced relationship;

6. use the ancient models as your model.

An artist is aware of being an instrument, not of being the creator. One famous ink and pen artist was noted for digging his fingers deep into the brush before starting to work. When asked why he did this he replied that only by doing this could he feel the ch'i in him travel down his arm, into the brush and thus on to the paper. The artist is a channel for the Tao and is expressing the flow of ch'i within all life through the creation of external expressions of this flow. It is this fundamental rootedness in something greater which gives Chinese art its highly distinctive appeal in its ability to combine activity with a sense of peacefulness, of harmonising the material and the spiritual.

The six principles of Hsieh Ho can be taken as a basic set of principles for creative life in general. You might be an artist, a dancer, an actor, creative in cooking or embroidery, skilful in writing, in poetry or in music. Or, indeed, you might just be a good amateur in any of these fields. Whatever you are, use of the six principles offers a guided meditational way of viewing, interacting and creating in a yin yang way.

Try using these six principles in relation to any activity which you do which you consider creative. You will find it can help turn a pastime into a meditational interaction with yourself, the materials you use and, through these, with the Tao of life itself. Remember, in Chinese thought, the whole universe is caught up in any aspect of creation. Therefore to be creative is to partake of creation itself.

For example, let's say you are a gardener. This is how you might use the six principles: First, be calm. Go into the garden to look, hear, feel. Let the garden reveal itself to you. Spend time atuning to what is and what might be. Becoming part of the garden, not some god, *deus ex machina*, who erupts upon the scene.

Secondly, begin to plan. Have an overall vision of what you wish to achieve so that all your actions build up to something greater than just the sum of your actions.

Thirdly, be realistic and excited by the limitations as well as the possibilities of what you have. If it is a tiny space, don't plant an oak tree! If it is a shady garden, don't plant flowers that need sunlight. Be visionarily realistic!

Fourthly, recognise you are contributing to what already is, what already exists. Do not bring in that which fundamentally clashes. So if you have an old wall, look for plants that reflect and respect the mellowness of the old stone. But if it's a concrete garage, cover it with colour.

Fifthly, see all parts in the whole. Look to balance colour with space; perhaps earth with water – a pond or fountain. Tall with short; round with thin. You can create a microcosm of the universe in your own garden.

Finally, be humble enough to learn from others.

MUSIC AND HARMONY

Music has an even greater role than art in the harmonising and balancing of the world. In some of the earliest texts of China, books such as *Shih Ching* and the *Chun Chiu* ('Book of Poetry' and the 'Spring and Autumn Annals', c.7th century BC), the gift of the musical notes is itself a result of harmony. The notes of classical Chinese music were believed to have been revealed through natural elements, and the right playing and combining of them was one of the ritual performances by the Confucianists and by the court which helped keep the world attuned. So sacred were these notes and so vital to the well-being of existence, that they were religious objects. Sets of bells, tuned to capture exactly each of the five notes and eight classifications of sound, were produced by the court and sent to the different provinces. There they were kept in the main Confucian temple and their accuracy was regularly tested, for if one of them were to be attuned wrong, then the world was out of order.

In the *Tso Chuan*, a 4th to 3rd century BC commentary on the *Chun Chiu*, the writer places music within a cosmic balance and harmony of heaven, earth and humanity:

Ceremonies constitute the standard of Heaven, the principle of Earth and the conduct of man. Heaven and Earth have their standards, and men take these as their

extremely interested
barroom(?) observe
– tolerance ???

*pattern, imitating the brilliant bodies of Heaven and
according with the natural diversities of Earth ... These
conditions produce the five tastes, make manifest the
five colours, and make evident the five notes. When
these are in excess, obscurity and confusion ensue, and
the people lose their original natures.*

*Therefore ceremonials were framed to reinforce this.
The nine songs, the winds of the eight directions, the
seven sounds and the six pitch-pipes were made to
maintain the five notes.*

The Confucian view of music is that, together with proper
conduct, which means not just moral behaviour but also
carrying out the right rituals at the right time, the world can
be kept in balance. Too much of either, or one or other
performed at the wrong time, can cause disruption in the
cosmic balance. So central was music to the Confucian and
pre-Confucian sense of being in harmony with nature, that
one of the earliest official classics was the *Classic of Music*
– now sadly lost. Hsun Tzu, a 3rd century BC philosopher
whose impact upon the development of Confucianism was
considerable, commented upon the significance of music in
reflections based upon the *Classic of Music*:

*When music is performed in the ancestral temple of the
ruler, and the ruler and his ministers, superiors and
inferiors, listen to it together, there are none who are
not filled with a spirit of harmonious reverence. When
it is performed within the household, and father and
sons, elder and younger brothers listen to it together,
there are none who are not filled with a spirit of
harmonious kinship. And when it is performed in the
community, and old people and young together listen to
it, there are none who are not filled with a spirit of
harmonious obedience. Hence music brings about
complete unity and induces harmony ... it is sufficient
to lead men in the single Way [Tao] or to bring order to
ten thousand charges [all life].*

This was not just a Confucian approach either. Taosim follows a similar understanding. In *Chuang Tzu* (chapter 14) there is a section on music which shows a Taoist view of music. The emperor is talking about why he performed a special kind of music. One of his ministers says:

'My Lord, *when you had the music performed in the area around Lake Tung Ting, I listened and at first I was afraid; I listened again and I was weary; I listened to the end and I was bewildered. I became upset and incapable of coherent speech and finally I lost my self assurance.'*

The Yellow Emperor said, 'That is what I would expect! Perfect music must first of all find its response in the world of the people. It must conform to the principles of Heaven and walk with the five Virtues. It should merge with spontaneity; as a result of which it can order the sequence of the four seasons, bring great harmony to all life. This will be seen in the procession of the four seasons, bringing all life to birth. At one moment swelling, at one declining, constrained by both martial and civil boundaries. At one moment clear, at one obscure, the yin and yang are in harmony, the sounds pour forth.

'*Next I played it with the harmony of yin and yang, and illuminated it by the light of the sun and moon. The notes filled the valleys and the gorges, and it was useless for you to try to block them out or protect your spirit, for such notes move as they wish. I stopped when the music stopped but the sounds flowed on. This worried you; you could not understand it; you looked for them, but could not see them; you went after them, but could not find them. You were stunned and so you stood before the universal witness of the Tao or leaned against an old tree and groaned. Your eyes could not understand and so failed you; your strength collapsed beneath you. I could not catch it. Your body dissolved into emptiness and you lost control and so achieved release. It was this which wore you out.*

'In the final section, I used notes that did not wear you out. I brought them together spontaneously. Some call this death, others life. Some call it fruit, others the flower. The notes moved, flowed, separated and changed, following no clear pattern. Understandably, the world is uncertain about them. The world sought advice from the sages, believing the sage to know true shape and true fate. "Listening for it, you do not hear it; looking for it you do not see its shape. It fills all Heaven and Earth, embracing the six directions." You desire to hear it, but it is beyond you, which is what confused you.

'I first performed the music which would induce awe, and because of this awe, fear arose like some spectre. Next I came up with weariness and this weariness brought on compliance in you. I ended with confusion and this made you feel stupid. But this stupidity reveals the Tao, the Tao that can be carried with you, wherever you are.'

For Chuang Tzu, music is capable of creating harmony at a variety of levels and of speaking, almost literally, of the relationship between yin and yang, heaven and earth and humanity's place within all this. For example, the eight sounds were seen to reflect the essential aspects of nature from which different sounds could be produced. The eight sounds were seen to arise from stone (reflected in a stone chime); metal (bronze bell); silk (zither); bamboo (flute); wood (pestle-and-mortar); skin (drum); gourd (mouth-organ); earth (vessel-flute). The five notes are do, re, mi, so, la, and each is believed to be the distillation of an element.

The strict rules regulating music arose precisely because it was felt to be so powerful. Chinese music sounds to a Western ear very harsh and discordant. Yet, to a Chinese ear, each note and its relationship to the next one is as with the five elements. Notes can create or destroy in relationship to other notes. Hsun Tzu sees the function of proper and improper music as cosmic in its significance:

*When music is moderate and tranquil, the people
become harmonious and shun excess. When music is
stern and majestic, the people become well behaved and
shun disorder ... But if music is seductive and
depraved, then the people will become abandoned and
mean mannered. Those who are abandoning will fall
into disorder.*

The role of music as both ordained by the Tao and as being
necessary for the well-being of the state is also rather
charmingly spelt out by Hsun Tzu. He argues that the
poeple have emotions of joyfulness and anger. If they have
no acceptable means of expressing this, then they become
rebellious and discontented. Music provides a safe and
essential means by which these emotions can be expressed
and thus released, in a confined and controlled way.
Without music, he argues, there would be disorder. With
music, reflecting as it does the very pattern of the Tao, there
comes harmony and tranquility.

BUILDING IN BALANCE

In chapter 3 we have already looked at the art of feng shui.
The relationship between human constructions and the
natural world – the realm of architecture, of town and city
planning, of interior and exterior design – is one of the most
important aspects of the search for balance and harmony in
Chinese life. The balance struck by using feng shui tech-
niques is clearly seen in Chinese art. The fine relationship
between buildings and their environment – the temple on an
outcrop of rock above a valley, the bridge over the river, the
small town nestled into the folds of a hill, the layout of the
imperial city – all these speak of a search for balance and
harmonious co-existence, and are reflected in Chinese art.
Even the very material of art itself has a role in the yin yang
balance of the home. Thus, in the women's quarters, porce-
lain, seen as a yin material, would be painted with yin type

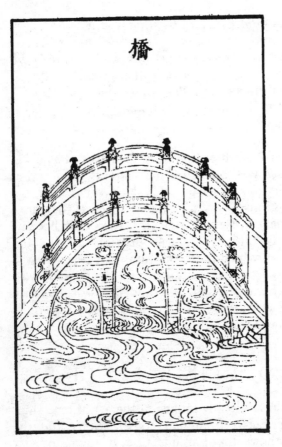

The bridge over the river depicts the search for balance and harmonious co-existence

illustrations – types of flower, water, goddesses – in order to increase the yin-ness of the women there.

THE *I CHING*: WINDOW INTO THE SOUL OF ART

Finally there is the role of the *I Ching* in art. This cannot be over-stated. The *I Ching* has acted as the metaphor bank, the divinational repository and the handbook to life's meaning for the Chinese for nearly three thousand years. Its images have infiltrated every aspect of traditional Chinese life.

Many Chinese paintings or sculptures are in fact figurative representations of the changes of the hexagrams (see pp. 96–101). As the hexagrams themselves are seen as manifestations of yin and yang through the combination of broken or continuous lines, each hexagram expresses these values and each hexagram is capable of being reversed. That is to say, if you exchange the yin lines for yang and vice versa, the hexagram becomes its opposite. Thus Chien – all yang lines, becomes Kun – all yin lines. Hexagram 49, Ke, predominantly yang, becomes hexagram 25, Wu Wang, predominantly yin.

Each trigram and each hexagram has characteristics associated with it, which, when portrayed in art, need to be matched. Thus the yang of 49 needs to be matched with the yin of 25. Once you know the associations, much of Chinese art begins to open up as an interplay between the hexagrams or the trigrams, an interplay in other words between yin and yang from which the harmony of the whole is constructed. The list sets out below the details in brief for the trigrams and for the hexagrams. You might like to try your own detective work on Chinese art to see which hexagrams are included in any painting.

A Key to Your Self

The insights into yin and yang which arise from the following lists of trigrams and hexagrams are also a key into your own self. By using the *I Ching* to obtain a trigram and then a hexagram, you can attune yourself to the flow of yin and yang. By then looking at what is around you and finding its reflection in one of the hexagrams, you can begin to assess whether you dwell in a yin or yang environment. Through balancing the yin or yang influences around you with art objects which increase the opposite force – yin and yang – you can create a beautiful and harmonious environment, just as Chinese art tries to do within itself. Through use of these insights you can widen this by not just looking at a piece of art as an expression of the balance of yin and yang, but looking at yourself, in relation to the art, as an expression of yin and yang.

To obtain a reading from the *I Ching*, you need an *I Ching*. We recommend *I Ching: The Shamanic Oracle of Change* (see bibliography).

There are two standard ways to obtain a reading.

1. The Three Coin System

Take three coins and throw them down together. Each throw creates a line. The 'tails' side is yang; the 'heads' side is yin. 'Tails' equals three points while 'heads' equals two points. So, if all three coins show 'tails', this equals yang – nine points. If all three coins are 'heads', this equals yin – six points. Two yin and one yang equals seven and two yang and one yin equals eight. This gives you:

Six = – – (yin line)

Seven = – – (yin line)

Eight = — (yang line)

Nine = — (yang line)

By three throws you create a trigram; six throws makes your hexagram. This you then find using the charts in the *I Ching*, which gives you your reading. However, note that lines of six or nine points can be interchanged – yin for yang or vice versa, thus producing another hexagram. Refer to both.

2. Pa Chien System

This uses eight coins, one marked in some way. Shuffle the coins, then lay them out around the eight trigrams starting with Chien – the all yang one – and then go clockwise.

The marked coin indicates one of the trigrams. This forms the bottom of your hexagram. Do the same again to find the trigram that marks the top three lines of your hexagram.

Trigrams

CHIEN father • dragon • horse • heaven • element/metal • late autumn • early night • deep red • head • strength • force • roundness.

KUN mother • mare • ox • earth • element/earth • later summer • early autumn • afternoon • people • black • abdomen • docility • nurturing • squareness.

CHEN eldest son • galloping horse or flying dragon • thunder • element/wood • spring • morning • young men • dark yellow • foot • movement • speed • roads • vegetables such as bamboo shoots.

KAN second son • pig • moon and fresh water • element/water • mid-winter • midnight • thieves • blood red • ear • danger • recklessness • curves.

KEN youngest son • dog • rat • birds with large beaks • mountain • element/wood • early spring • early morning • gate-keepers • no colour associated • hand and finger • mountain passes • gates • fruits and seeds.

SUN eldest daughter • hen • wind • element/wood • late spring • early summer • morning • merchants • white • thigh • slow and steady • plants growing.

LI second daughter • pheasant • toad • crab • snail • tortoise • lightning • element/fire • summer • mid-day • amazons • no colour associated • eye • weapons • dry trees • drought.

TUI youngest daughter or concubine • sheep • sea and salt water • elements/water and metal • mid-autumn • evening • enchantress • no colour associated • mouth and tongue • reflections and mirror images • death scenes.

Hexagrams

1. CHIEN heaven • father • king • controlling forces.

2. KUN earth • mother • people • docile • subordinate.

3. CHUN initial problems.

4. MENG youthful inexperience.

5. HSU deliberately holding back • delaying.

6. SUNG arguing in law courts • litigation.

7. SHIH military manoeuvres or army officers.

8. PI union and agreement.

9. HSIAO CHU creative powers being tamed or controlled.

10. LI walking carefully • on an edge.

11. TAI springtime • peace.

12. PI start of autumn.

13. TUNG JEN community • harmony.

14. TA YU opulence • excess of goods.

15. CHIEN hidden wealth • modesty.

16. YU excitement • enthusiasm.

17. SUI following on behind.

18. KU struggling against decay and collapse.

19. LIN figures of authority approaching.

20. KUAN sitting contemplating • asking for oracles • divination.

21. SHI HO crowds • markets • courts and lawyers.

22. PI ornaments.

23. PO falling • overthrowing or collapsing – especially a house.

24. FU New Year's Eve.

25. WU WANG cautiously.

26. TA CHU creative forces held down by that which is immobile.

27. I mouth.

28. TA KUO something large and unusual but not unpleasant.

29. KAN cliff edge with rushing water below.

30. LI a net or the interplay of fire and light.

31. HSIAN interweaving.

32. HENG perseverance.

33. TUN withdrawing • retreat.

34. TA CHUANG great strength.

35. CHIN rising and advancing.

36. MING I a good person being turned away or rejected.

37. CHIA JEN members of a family.

38. KUEI division and alienation.

39. CHIEN lameness or being restricted in some way.

40. CHIAI unravelling • releasing.

41. SUN taking away too much of something • taxes.

42. I adding to something.

43. KUAI breaking through • releasing from tension.

44. KOU sexual intercourse • meeting between the sexes.

45. TSUI communion · gathering together for a common purpose.

46. SHENG the successful career of an official.

47. KUN surrounded and bewildered.

48. CHING a well · dependable.

49. KE moulting skins.

50. TING food.

51. CHEN thunder or earthquake · moving forces.

52. KEN stability · mountain.

53. CHIEN dyeing · changing colours · slow changes.

54. KUEI MEI marriage.

55. FENG prosperity and abundance.

56. LU travellers · strangers and merchants.

57. SUN windswept and blasted.

58. TUI sea and delight.

59. HUAN scattering and being cut off.

60. CHIEH joints of bamboo • regulation • reflection • meditation.

61. CHUNG FU inner serenity • kingly authority.

62. HSIAO KUO small details and miniature versions of things.

63. CHI CHI finished • completed • achieved.

64. WEI CHI unfinished.

Using these codes, it is possible to examine Chinese art anew, and to see the interplay between yin and yang.

YOU IN ART

Ultimately, what Chinese arts – painting, music, sculpture, and so forth – are about is balance and finding your place, your meaning, your purpose in the ever-changing world around you. You are not the observer. You are part of the process and to understand that process you need to decode the images, unlock the symbolism and enter into the flow of Tao, be that through a pen and ink drawing or through the preparation of a simple balanced meal (see chapter 4). No action is outside the yin yang dynamic. No action is without its significance for either harmony and balance, or chaos and distress. You are the pivot around which the whole revolves and you are also but one aspect of a greater whole.

In using the six principles, in looking at paintings and at life through the lens of the symbolism of the *I Ching*, by seeking dynamic examples of harmony from difference in colours, styles and shapes, you can learn to see an old familiar world anew. What Chinese art does is to ask you to stop looking at and become part of. It asks you to drop the traditional Western way of relating to art – standing back from it. Instead it invites you to enter into it, to lose yourself in it.

And this does not just apply to formal art. This is in essence about the art of living itself. Formal art simply shows us in particular modes and in specific materials what the whole of life should be about.

The yin and yang of art is an enactment of the reality of the cosmos in the details of ordinary life. This is in truth the heart of yin yang wisdom.

6

Walking the Way of the Tao: Yin and Yang in Our Future

THE SEARCH FOR HARMONY

THE CHINA CREATED by the theory of yin and yang, by the pursuit of harmony and balance, has largely collapsed. In part this was because the practice never lived up to the theory. As we saw in chapter 4, officially women were seen as lesser beings – not quite the model of yin and yang as equals. Much of the pursuit of balance and harmony was only possible for the wealthy. For the poor, the overwhelming mass of the people of China throughout the ages, the possibilities of harmony and balance were greatly restricted by the sheer struggle to survive.

Yet in even the poorest family, the search for balance and harmony made and continues to make its mark. Where dietary balance can be afforded, many Chinese will practise it instinctively. At major festivals and rites of passage such as weddings, the symbols and assumptions of yin and yang (e.g. dragon and phoenix symbols at weddings – representing yang and yin) will have their place. Walk early in the morning in the streets of China and you will see people of all ages practising breathing exercises, designed to move the ch'i around the body and to balance the body overall. Even feng shui is reappearing in China, albeit often on environmental grounds rather than any quasi-philosophical, religious basis.

But much of the beauty that was the hallmark of physical China has been destroyed or is being destroyed. Once proud and beautiful cities have been Stalinised and Maoified with vast grey buildings and endless highrise blocks of cheap housing. What is left is now being 'modernised' in the name of free enterprise. Old grid plans with their feng shui alignments or ancient temples with their power of yin and yang regeneration have been swept away by the march of utilitarian city planning.

In some areas, however, the old theory has never waned. Medicine is one such area, though it too has had to shed much of its religio-philosophical dress in order to survive.

THE BALANCE OF NATURE

Certain lessons have been learnt, even if under traditional Chinese wisdom they need never have been experimented with in the first place. The balance of nature has been drastically disturbed. For example, the purge in 1962 of all birds in cities led to the slaughter of thousands of millions of birds. The result was that for years afterwards the cities were infested with insects as their natural predators had been wiped out. On a larger scale, the disastrous pollution of the main cities is now being recognised as a problem of monumental scale – so much so that even Deng Xiao Ping's daughter addressed this issue forthrightly at a conference held in Peking on the environment in July 1995. This would have been inconceivable five years previously because such criticism of the industrial advance of China would have been viewed as treason.

It is just possible that China may recover its yin and yang, harmony and balance model before it destroys everything of its past. One of its complaints against the West is that only rich countries can have the luxury of such a quest for balance and harmony – forgetting or ignoring its own past.

There is some truth in this. In the post-industrial countries of the West, we now have the time and to some extent the ability to look again at how we relate to the environment; to each other; to ourselves. And in doing so, many people are finding that the Chinese understanding of all these relationships and more, in terms of yin and yang, is of immense benefit.

We have torn much of our world apart through the search for security and peace in our lives. Reliance upon material goods, on miracle cures for illnesses, of specialists to help us put our lives together again or to imbue them with meaning, have all actually led to a great sense of alienation. We have a greater feeling of being alone and against everything, or of having a greater sense of what we ought to be worth, than society, our lives and work actually can give us.

The yin and yang, harmony and balance theory will not cure all those ills. But it does offer another way of viewing reality which might just help to jump start us back on to a more liveable way of life.

The Environment

We have treated the natural world as little more than raw resources and a dumping ground. Then we are surprised when the natural systems begin to collapse, and when pollution brings in its wake illnesses and problems that make life a misery. We have behaved as if we were separate from the rest of nature, onlookers, in the same way that we see ourselves as onlookers to a painting. We have disturbed balances, released poisons into water, filled the air with toxins and then expressed astonishment that this makes us ill.

Look again at what we are doing, but through the eyes of balancing the yin and yang forces, of going with the flow of the Tao. Much of what we do is designed to disrupt the natural course of nature. The Chinese have never lacked the ability to develop. They have experimented, developed, innovated and produced as much as any other great culture, possibly more so. Yet they have in the past tried to do so in balanced relationship to the rest of nature. The art of feng shui shows this perhaps at its clearest.

What if we were to look at our use of the natural environment in this light? What if we were to look at the environment as something within which humanity needs to find a balance with the rest of creation, as a world in which the consequences of our actions have to be accepted – either through not doing that which we know to destroy the balance, or by making amends? In the past the emperor went each year, first to the temple of heaven and then to the temple of earth, to apologise to, seek a renewal of relationship with and offer guidance for, nature. Maybe a new form of such humility combined with recognition of our key role in nature is needed. Instead of, or perhaps as well as, great conferences and worthy plans, we need to apologise to nature and to restore or rebuild our relationship with the rest of life on earth. If this seems too much, at least we need some way of acknowledging that this relationship has gone terribly, terribly wrong.

Personal Relationships

On the level of personal relationships, the notion of the feminine within the masculine and the masculine within the feminine owes a great deal to the discovery of the yin yang symbol, even if it has often been rather naïvely expressed. One major misunderstanding of the yin yang model is the ignoring of conflict. For most people in the West, harmony means no conflict and peace means an absence of violence, but these two states are unachievable. The true meaning of yin and yang is that there is always the potential if not the reality of conflict, struggle, difference, diversity and violence – verbal, structural or military. What the Chinese look for in their model of harmony and balance is to hold these powerful forces in dynamic tension, recognising that the difference and struggle is what gives birth to the energy, but also acknowledging that this energy can destroy itself unless a balance is found.

Conflict resolution, not trying to pretend that conflict either doesn't exist or will go away, is what the yin yang symbol is all about. The rise and fall of powers, the ebbing and flowing of forces, is as natural as the rise of winter, declining into spring, giving rise to summer, which itself declines into autumn to give way to winter again.

In personal relationships, the waxing and waning of yin and of yang offers a key to understanding the complexities of our own natures and of those around us. Trying to be all yang – macho, emotionless, hard and determined – is, according to classic yin yang theory, foolish because at the very moment of supreme yangness, the yin begins to rise and thus all will change. Trying to suppress the yin within the yang leads only to distress and confusion because it will manifest itself somehow.

Likewise, trying to be all yin – weak and helpless, emotional, dependent – is foolish because this is destructive as well. The yang is there and to deny it is to store up troubles for the future. It is unhealthy to try and be just one aspect of the twin forces of the Tao.

In reverse, those who are predominantly yang, male, should not try to become more yin, to become weak and helpless. Nor should those who are predominantly yin, female, become more yang than the yang. Weak men and hard women are anathema to the yin yang model. Instead a balance between that which predominates in us, be that yin or yang, and that which is contained within that which predominates, be that yang or yin, is what should be sought. In any relationship, couples should learn to understand who is the predominantly yin and who is the predominantly yang. This is not tied to sexuality. A man might be the more yin person in a relationship, with the woman more yang. Such a discovery can lead to a better understanding of different roles and needs within a relationship. Balancing what is there already with either what you wish to develop in your relationship or what you need to handle with care because of its destructiveness, can help to deepen and mature such relationships, recognising both the good, the bad and the indifferent within such partnerships and within each of us.

Understanding Who We Are

In terms of ourselves, understanding what makes us who we are is central to the balance and harmony of ourselves. Reflecting upon our personality and trying to understand or interpret it in terms of yin and yang, of the five elements, of forces at work within and upon us, helps to make the tensions and frustrations, as well as the energies and joys of our lives, more intelligible. We are not just one thing. We are ourselves, diversity in action, difference within one human frame. Handling and exploring these diversities within us helps us to live with what our own culture often tells us are irreconcilable opposites. They are not. They are simply the outworkings of the fact that we are all both yin and yang, and that to deny this or to expect only one to be present is both foolish and, according to Taoist teachings, dangerous.

Handling the contradictions within us by not seeing them as contradictions but as part and parcel of who we are is often a great relief to people in the West. We have been told that such 'contradictions' are unacceptable or disturbing. They are only if you see them as contradictions rather than as aspects of two forces, two opposed and struggling forces, at work within not just you, but all life. Learning to accept this and to see this as perfectly natural is what lies at the heart of the Chinese concept of personality. It is one which has much to offer Westerners trapped in an either/or mentality, one which denies diversity within.

In terms of creating a living space, be that for work or for home, the teachings of feng shui offer much that can help you to make a space your own by reflecting to you what your own yin or yang dominated personality needs to balance and calm it, and to provide a space to exist within.

The same is true about health and diet. By looking for a more balanced and balancing diet it is certainly possible to help yourself to a fitter and more consistent pattern of health. The avoidance of excess and the harmonising of different needs is of core importance. Understanding why certain cravings for more yang or more yin food arises, and allowing some indulgence of that followed by balancing it with the opposite, means that you walk a proper line between over-indulgence and over-asceticism.

THE WAY OF NATURE

But perhaps the most important aspect of the relation of yin and yang to yourself, to your relationships, to your society and culture and to your planet is that all this is but part of the Tao, part of the way of nature. It is this above all else that places us and our world in perspective. We are the third leg of the triad of heaven, earth and humanity. We have a vital role. Yet our vital role is simply yet gloriously to ensure that the two forces of heaven and earth, yin and yang, are able to continue to be in balanced relationship with each other. Through this balancing, we have our central position which makes us feel we have a place in the universe, a meaning in the cosmos. But recognising that that place is there not to glorify humanity, but to serve the rest of life, is essential. Due humility before the awe-ful-ness of the Tao comes from the security of knowing that we are part of the Tao and that we are secure within that.

If Jung was right in saying that we have to have myths or stories of our place in the universe because without some sense of who and what we are we would be crushed by the sheer awe-ful-ness of the unknown, then it is equally important that we understand what those myths or stories are telling us. In the West we veer between the biblical story with its central and at times almost supreme role for human beings, to the insignificance that comes from knowing that we inhabit an unimportant planet circling an obscure star in a corner of a modest galaxy in the Milky Way.

In the story of yin and yang we, as human beings, have a role which in an interesting way holds together the best and most significant aspects of the two Western stories – our centrality and our part in something bigger. However, all this comes without the issue of a creator god or the anonymity of a chance universe.

In finding a place for ourselves within the purpose of change which is the Tao; in recognising that change is the fundamental nature of the Tao; in seeing diversity and opposition as inherent and essential within the way of nature and of the universe; in finding within ourselves the two opposite forces at work, in conflict and in creative dynamic, Chinese philosophy has offered us a model which can help us live with ourselves, with each other and within the universe. That this neither requires of us a belief in god nor a denial of god is undoubtably a bonus. But, most important of all, it offers us a way to hold in tension the diversity of ourselves, of our world and of life itself. This is the balancing harmony of the Tao.

Bibliography/Sources

(page 6) extract from *The Doctrine of the Mean*, quoted on page 146 of *Sources of Chinese Civilisation, Vol. I*, edited by Wm.Theodore de Bary, Columbia University Press, New York, 1960

(pages 7, 29) *Tao Te Ching*, translated by Man-Ho Kwok, Martin Palmer and Jay Ramsay, Element, 1993

(pages 7, 8, 58, 83, 90) *Chuang Tzu*, translated by Martin Palmer and Elizabeth Breuilly, Arkana, 1995

(pages 14, 53) *The Yellow Emperor's Classic of Internal Medicine (Book 2)*, translated by Ilza Veith, University of California Press, Berkeley, 1972

(page 16) *Ch'un ch'iu fan-lu*, 59, Tung Chung Shu, adapted from the translation in *Sources of Chinese Civilisation, Vol. I*, edited by Wm. Theodore de Bary, Columbia University Press, New York, 1960

(page 18) *Chinese Face and Hand Reading*, Man-Ho Kwok and Joanne O'Brien, Chinese Popular Classics, Piatkus, 1995

(page 27) *Book of Master Huai Nan*, Chapter 7, 3a-1 to 3b-3 taken from *Taoism and the Rite of Cosmic Renewal*, Michael Saso, second edition, Washington State University Press, Washington, 1989

(page 28) *Chi Ni Tzu*, translation from page 555 of *Science and Civilisation, Vol. II*, Joseph Needham, Cambridge University Press, 1956

(page 57) *Chinese Medicine*, Ted Kaptchuk, Rider Books, 1983

(page 58) *Pao Pu Tzu*, Chapter 5 – quoted in the *Taoist Statement On Nature*, Beijing, 1995

(page 59) *Ku chi huan shen chiu chuan chiung tan lun*, 'The study of the path for affirming the breath and causing the soul

YIN AND YANG

to return' quoted on page 87 of *Taoist Meditation – the Mao-Shan Tradition of Great Purity*, Isabelle Robinet, State University of New York Press, New York, 1993

(page 61) Extract adapted from the translation given on pages 51–112 of *Taoism and Chinese Religion*, Henri Maspero, translated by Frank A. Kierman, Jr, University of Massachusetts Press, 1981

(page 68) *I Ching*, translation taken from *Sacred Books of the East, Vol. 16*, James Legge, Oxford, 1899

(page 74) *Tso Chuan*, quoted in *A History of Chinese Philosophy, Vol. I*, Fung Yu-Lan, Princeton University Press, 1952

(page 75) 'Priceless Recipe', quoted in Jack Santa Maria's *Chinese Vegetarian Cooking*, Rider, 1983

(page 80) Extract of Tsung Ping taken from page 253 of *Sources of Chinese Civilisation, Vol. I*, edited by Wm. Theodore de Bary, Columbia University Press, New York, 1960

(page 85) Chang Tsai, quoted in Tu Wei Ming's essay 'The Continuity of Being' in *Nature in Asian Traditions of Thought*, edited by J. Baird Callicott and Roger T. Ames, State University of New York Press, New York, 1989

(page 87) Extract from the *Tso Chuan*, quoted on page 38, Fung Yu-lan's *A History of Chinese Philosophy, Vol. I*, Princeton University Press, 1952

(pages 88, 91) Section 20 of *Hsun Tzu*, 'Classic of Music', translated by Burton Watson, Columbia University Press, 1963

(page 94) I *Ching: The Shamanic Oracle of Change*, translated by M. Palmer, J, Ramsay and X. Zhao, Thorsons, 1995

Index